Lt Col (Retired) George Forty, OBE, FMA, is a well-known military historian. He was born in London in 1927 and commissioned into the Royal Tank Regiment in July 1948, the first post-war intake from Sandhurst when it reopened. He went on to serve in the Korean War, being wounded in action in May 1953, whilst commanding a troop of tanks during the Hook battle. He then served all over the world including Aden, the Persian Gulf, Borneo and Germany. He retired in 1977 after 32 years, to begin a writing career, but in 1981, was appointed Director/Curator of the world famous Tank Museum in Bovington, Dorset, retiring in 1994, being awarded the OBE and made a Fellow of the Museums Association. He then became editor of TANK, the Regimental Journal of the RTR, retiring for a third time in 2010. He and his wife, Anne, have lived in Briantspuddle for the past 31 years. They have four sons and nine grandchildren.

IN THE SAME SERIES

DORSET: The Royal Air Force
Colin Pomeroy

DORSET: The Royal Navy
Stuart Morris

FOLLOWING PAGE
A recruiting advertisement from the *Dorset County Chronicle* shortly
after the start of the First World War in 1914.

4th BATT. DORSET REGIMENT.

MEN OF DORSET !
Your King and Country Need You.

JOIN YOUR
COUNTY BATTALION

In consequence of 600 Non-Commissioned Officers and Men of the 4th Dorsets (Territorials) having

Volunteered for Foreign Service,

500 RECRUITS

Are now needed to complete the Establishment, and

600 RECRUITS
FOR HOME SERVICE.

Officer Commanding.

DORSET

THE ARMY

GEORGE FORTY

THE DOVECOTE PRESS

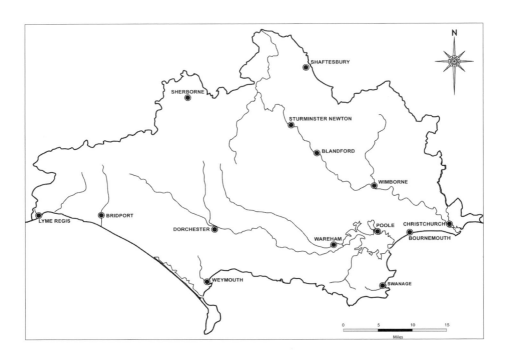

First published in 2011 by The Dovecote Press Ltd
Stanbridge, Wimborne Minster, Dorset BH21 4JD

ISBN 978-1-904-34989-1

© George Forty 2011
George Forty has asserted his rights under the Copyright, Designs
and Patent Act 1988 to be identified as author of this work

Typeset in FS Ingrid and designed by The Dovecote Press Ltd
Printed and bound by GraphyCems, Navarra

All papers used by The Dovecote Press are natural, recyclable products
made from wood grown in sustainable, well-managed forests.

A CIP catalogue record for this book is available from the British Library

CONTENTS

ONE

SAXONS TO SEDGEMOOR

THE FYRD

Evidence of anything remotely resembling a Dorset-based 'army' did not really appear until the formation of the Saxon fyrd, which is first mentioned in the 'Anglo-Saxon Chronicle' of AD 605. However, it was King Alfred, who, some 200 years later, galvanised the Saxons into producing an effective fighting force in his struggles with the Vikings. Local in character, the Fyrd was a militia of able-bodied freemen, aged from 16 to 60, who were only assembled when war threatened, otherwise they lived a normal life, working on their farms. It was they who helped Alfred defend Bridport, Shaftesbury and Wareham – the three Dorset towns he fortified.

After 1066, with the birth of the feudal system, the Normans introduced mounted knights, and their auxiliaries (infantry and military artisans), whilst mercenaries were employed in combination with the militia during the Hundred Years War and the Wars of the Roses. Dorset became an important centre for the manufacture of longbows. In 1346, the year of the Battle of Crecy, six towns in Dorset and Somerset manufactured some 11,000 arrows and delivered them to Bristol, corded together for stowage in wooden tuns that were stacked in carts and wagons hired for the purpose.

TRAINED BANDS OR MILITIA

The system did not change until the reign of Queen Elizabeth I when the Trained Bands made their appearance. They were a local militia organised within counties for the defence of the realm by the Lord Lieutenants, who employed professional soldiers to teach the rudiments of drill, and the use of such weapons as pikes and muskets. Membership was compulsory for all freeholders, householders and their sons – in other words, men who had a stake in the county and were thus expected to defend it against foreign invasion or insurrection. Some freemen would hire 'stand-ins' to attend the training sessions that were held monthly during the summer.

With no regular army, the militia were the only semi-permanent military units in the seventeenth century. It was not until the beginning of the eighteenth century that the first proper regiments of foot and horse were formed, eventually becoming the designated county regiments.

James, Duke of Monmouth.   John Churchill, 1st Duke of Marlborough.

THE MONMOUTH REBELLION

In June 1685, the Duke of Monmouth, an illegitimate son of Charles II, landed at Lyme Regis in a doomed attempt to win the throne. Once safely ashore, the Duke gathered a small army, clashing with the Dorset militia at Bridport. West Dorset proved an important recruiting ground for the rebel force, limiting the effectiveness of the militia. Two of its officers were killed, one was mortally wounded, and two more was forced to hide, one in an attic, the other in a plot of kidney beans. Shortly afterwards Monmouth declared himself king and was crowned at Chard.

In due course the various county militias were strengthened by James II's regular army. In command of the cavalry was John, Lord Churchill. Monmouth's force was no match for the disciplined Horse Guards and Royal Regiment of Dragoons. Within a month his rag-tag force of West Country farmers and tradesmen had been routed at the Battle of Sedgemoor, his rebellion had failed, and their luckless leader was found hiding in a ditch near Wimborne. The Duke was executed, 320 of his followers were condemned to death, and many more to transportation in the West Indies.

Sedgemoor was the last pitched battle to be fought on English soil, but perhaps the most important outcome of the Rebellion was the creation of a permanent professional standing army. New regiments were formed to counter the rebels, and though none was completed in time to take to the field at Sedgemoor, none was disbanded after the emergency was over.

TWO

THE 39th FOOT AND DORSETSHIRE REGIMENT

Twenty years later, John Churchill's part in the defeat of the Duke of Monmouth was eclipsed by his role as commander-in-chief at the first resounding victory by a British general on foreign soil since the Middle Ages. In 1705, by now Captain-General of the Army and 1st Duke of Marlborough, he defeated the French and Bavarians at the Battle of Blenheim. Other victories, at Ramillies and Malplaquet, followed. The prime instrument on which Marlborough relied was the British Army. Tested in William of Orange's military campagns against France in the 1690s, it had gradually expanded by doubling the establishments of existing regiments and raising new ones. During the course of the war 50 new regiments of foot, including marines, were added, of which those later numbered as the 28th-39th Foot survived the peace.

The last of these, the 39th, was the Dorsetshire Regiment of Foot which had originally been raised in Ireland in August 1702. The process by which regiments found their final form – and name – is complicated. For example, the 39th Foot was the reforming of Colonel Richard Coote's Regiment of Foot, which he had inherited ten years earlier from Viscount Lisburne's Regiment of Foot, originally formed in 1689. The 39th provided the first British troops in India, fighting successfully at Plassey in 1757 (hence their motto 'Primus in Indis'). In 1795, they

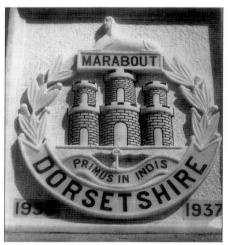

were reformed in Ireland, absorbing the short-lived 104th Regiment of Foot (Royal Manchester Volunteers).

A few years later a number of regiments had their territorial affiliations shuffled about, the East Middlesex title passed on to the 77th Foot, whilst the 39th took the 'Dorsetshire' title and

The cap badge of the Dorsteshire Regiment carved out of Agra marble, located at the Khyber Pass, on the North West Frontier, Pakistan. Marabout refers to the part played by the Regiment in the capture of Fort Marabout in Egypt in 1801.

Officers of the 39th Regiment of Foot in the late eighteenth century.

became The 39th (Dorsetshire) Regiment of Foot. With this title, the 39th were sent to Australia in 1825, seeing service in Hobart, Sydney, Swan River colony and Bathurst. They left in 1832 for further service in India, then, in 1881, they were amalgamated with the 54th (West Norfolk) Regiment and that same year the numerical regimental titles were abolished.

Also in 1881 the North Devonshire Regiment of Foot became became the Devonshire Regiment; the 39th (Dorsetshire) Regiment of Foot became the 1st Battalion the Dorsetshire Regiment, while the 54th (West Norfolk) Regiment of Foot became the 2nd Battalion, The Dorsetshire Regiment. Regimental Depots were established at Exeter and Dorchester. And so they remained through the Boer War and both World Wars until, in 1948, The Dorsetshire Regiment was renamed The Dorset Regiment.

The Dorsetshire Regiment spent much of the Victorian period stationed in India, and it was here that Lance Corporal Samuel Vickery was awarded the Victoria Cross for outstanding bravery during the Tirah campaign on the North West frontier, rescuing a wounded comrade under fire in October 1897. Tirah is near the Khyber Pass on what is now the Afghanistan/Pakistan border, and remains as hazardous today as it did then.

The Homecoming Reception for Samuel Vickery, VC, at the Southwestern station Dorchester, 17 June 1898. Vickery later served in South Africa during the Boer War and with the 6th Battalion in France during the First World War. His Victoria Cross is on display in the Keep Military Museum, Dorchester.

However, the amalgamations were not yet over and in 1958 came another one, this time with the Devonshire Regiment, to form the 'Devonshire and Dorset Regiment', a title that lasted for the next 50 years, during which time the Regiment, which was the senior County Regiment in the British Army, served in Cyprus, British Guiana (Guyana), Northern Ireland, West Germany, Malta, British Honduras (Belize), Berlin, the Falkland Islands, the Gulf, Bosnia, Iraq and Afghanistan.

Top Colours of the 1st Volunteer Battalion being laid up in Sherborne, 19 May 1901. In the background are Sherborne Abbey and the Digby Hotel.

Centre Men of 'G' Company, 1st Dorsets, returning to Camp over Wool Bridge, after manoeuvres on Salisbury Plain, 1909.

Bottom The band of the 4th Battalion, the Dorsetshire Regiment, in 1912.

THREE

THE DORSET RIFLE VOLUNTEERS

In 1859 Dorset was among selected counties whose Lord Lieutenants were authorised to set up volunteer groups. The result was the Dorset Rifle Volunteers, who after fighting in the Boer War (see Chapter 6) became an official part of the Territorials in 1908.

Above & below Men of the Dorset Rifle Volunteers in the 1870s. The photograph above is of No 3 Corps at West Walks, Dorchester, prior to a day on the rifle ranges.

Two views of the first annual camp of the Dorset Rifle Volunteers at West Lulworth in 1864. The camp was commanded by Colonel Mansel and lasted five days in July. It was the equivalent of the modern regimental open day, and wives and families were invited to watch the military abilities of their loved ones.

FOUR

THE DORSET YEOMANRY

DORSETSHIRE
Lord Milton desires the favour of the Gentlemen,
Yeomen and Farmers of the County of Dorset, to attend
either at DORCHESTER on Saturday the 3rd of May,
or at WINBOURNE on Friday the 9th of May, or at
BLANDFORD or WAREHAM, on Saturday the 10th of
May, as may best suit their Convenience, for the purpose
of Enrolling themselves in a Volunteer Corps of LIGHT
CAVALRY, to be formed for the Internal Defence of the
Country.
Dorchester Printed by Lockett, 1794.

Having seen service in the American War of Independence, Lord Milton, eldest son of the Earl of Dorchester, was unimpressed by the 'anti-invasion militia force' that turned out in late 1792 to answer the threat of invasion from Napoleonic France. He determined to form a 'Corps of Gentlemen and Yeomen' and approached the Secretary of State for War with a proposal to raise a volunteer force of light cavalry, at no expense to the Government. The force, he envisaged, would consist of a few score of foxhunting squires, each bringing two followers, yeomen farmers or estate servants, all mounted and equipped. Nothing much happened for about a year, but then he was informed that his scheme had been officially adopted and approved. Its principal purpose was to defend the coast and assist the regular army should invasion become a reality. It was officially named the Yeomanry Corps of Light Cavalry in the County of Dorset, but was more commonly called the Dorset Volunteer Rangers, or the DVR.

Greeted with enthusiasm, a substantial sum of over £1,425 was subscribed immediately to equip the Dorset contingent. Recruiting for six troops began at once, advertisements were circulated and by the following month training was well under way. The Government supplied a sword, pistol and holster per man, whilst the uniform, the horses and their saddlery were provided by the officers. The uniform was a dark green jacket and waistcoat, with yellow buttons (inscribed

Lord Milton, the first Colonel of the Dorset Volunteer Rangers.

'DVR') and black velvet upturned collar and cuffs, topped off with a round hat with a bearskin and green feathers. Training was a maximum of two days a week, but not during harvest or sheep shearing. The first regimental exercise was a parade at Poundbury on 8 May 1794.

King George III took a personal interest in the DVR, first inspecting them just four months after their formation and then again on three more occasions between 1798 and 1802. The 'Royal' Title was granted for services to Dowager Queen Adelaide.

No enemy landing was ever made on the Dorset coast, although the DVR did turn out to a number of false alarms towards the end of the eighteenth century. Probably the best example was when a Captain Daniel arrived half clothed at Weymouth, having swum his horse across the ferry passage at Smallmouth, with news that the French had landed on Portland. The DVR quickly assembled at Poxwell, where Major Frampton, temporarily in command, received a message that

The Dorset Volunteer Rangers was not the only force formed to counter the threat of invasion by France. Others included the Dorset Volunteers, whose three battalions numbered over 2,000 men in 1800; the Beaminster Loyal Town Volunteers; and the Royal Portland Legion. This engraving shows John Penn, the captain in command of the Royal Portland Legion, being handed a wheatear which has just been taken from the stone trap in the foreground. Penn, like the other two mounted officers, is wearing the uniform of the Legion. In 1804 it consisted of four officers, eight N.C.O.s, four drummers and 103 privates.

included the following: 'Capt Daniel said the French were landed in Portland and Capt Ingram (commander of the Sea Fencibles and Signal Houses at Weymouth) said that our Corps ought to assist in repelling them immediately. Weymouth is entirely in a state of Confusion and Uproar. Excuse this scrole written in Mr Damer's stable . . .' In addition to the DVR, the Weymouth Volunteers and two Regiments of Hanoverians (mercenaries raised in Hanover for the defence of England and disbanded in 1814) were also called out – and all for no reason. Tradition has it that the unfortunate Captain Daniel was misled by the return of the fishing fleet in a dense fog.

In April 1802 came peace and with it the option to carry on or stand down. Due to the continued threat of war with France, the DVR chose the latter, their officers offering to re-raise the DVR as the Dorset Yeomanry Cavalry. By the time war was declared in May 1803, the fledgling Dorset Yeomanry Cavalry was organised on a seven troop basis with over 500 all ranks. When re-raised they were also given permission to form independent troops, each with its own uniform. Five such troops were raised and later disbanded following the final defeat of the French at Waterloo in 1815.

Fifteen years later, in 1830, there were a number of disturbances throughout much of the south, known as the Swing Riots. Their livelihood threatened by the invention of the threshing machine, agricultural labourers began destroying the machines and setting fire to ricks. There were riots in Sherborne, Blandford, Sixpenny Handley, Winfrith and Corfe Castle. Fearful of further unrest, the Yeomanry was reformed in 1831 as a Corps of 600 officers and men, initially as

Members of the Princess Victoria's Regiment of Dorset Yeomanry Cavalry in 1835.

Princess Victoria's Regiment of Dorset Yeomanry Cavalry, and later as the Queen's Own Dorset Yeomanry. Also that year it was ruled that all cavalry, except for Horse Guards would wear red, so a new uniform was adopted of a scarlet jacket with silver lace collar and cuffs, black trousers with two scarlet stripes.

Lt Col W. E. Brymer, MP, inspecting B Squadron of the Dorset Yeomanry in Blandford Forum Market Place, May 1894, a painting by Roger Lowless.

The charge of the Dorset Yeomanry at the Battle of Agagia, 26 February 1916. The charge against 500 Senussi tribesmen with four machine guns under heavy fire across 1,200 yards of open desert effectively ended the Senussi revolt against British rule in Egypt. Of the 184 yeomen cavalry, 32 were killed. (The original of this painting by Lady Butler, hangs in the offices of the Dorset County Council and appears here by kind permission of the Chief Executive).

THE YEOMANRY GO TO WAR

The Boer War would provide the Yeomanry with the chance of serving overseas. The Queen's Own Dorset Yeomanry (QODY) was part of the 10,000 strong Imperial Yeomanry that supported the regular cavalry, fighting bravely in South Africa and also in the First World War, when three QODY Regiments were formed, the 1st/1st going to the Middle East, whilst the 1st/2nd and 1st/3rd both served in England then Ireland. The QODY's famous charge at Agagia remains one of the most historic cavalry charges of the First World War, and one of the last.

The Queen's Own Dorset Imperial Yeomanry going to War, 1914.

A CHANGE OF ROLE

Between the wars the Yeomanry was reduced, the ten most senior regiments being retained as cavalry, whilst the remainder had to choose between conversion (to field artillery, tanks, or reconnaissance) or disbandment. They chose the former, because in those days field artillery was still horse drawn. They became the 141st (QODY) Field Regiment RA, TA, and were mobilised on the outbreak of war in September 1939 and equipped with the new 25 pdr field guns. At annual camp in 1939, 400 new recruits attended and shortly afterwards, QODY was split into two regiments – 141 QODY Field Regiment (the two original yeomanry batteries) and 94th Hants & Dorset Field Regiment, both being part of the 43rd Wessex Division. 141st stayed in England, whilst 94th supported 129 Bde, 43rd Wessex Division, for the rest of the war.

After the war in Europe ended in May 1945, the 94th began occupational duties in Germany, acting as infantry once their guns were withdrawn, then, from April 1946, the men were sent home for demobilisation and disbandment.

In 1947 two TA towed Gunner Regiments were re-raised: 341st (QODY) Medium Regt RA, TA, armed with 5.5inch guns, with its HQ and one battery at Sherborne and the other battery split between Shaftesbury and Blandford; 294th (Dorset) Field Regt, RA, TA, armed with 25 pdrs, with its HQ and one battery at Dorchester, one at Bridport, one at Parkstone. A third Regiment (coastal artillery) was also re-raised and stationed in Weymouth, Poole and Portland. However, it soon became evident that the county could not man three RA regiments, so, in 1951, 341 and 294 were merged to form 294th (QODY) Fd Regt RA, TA, with its HQ and HQ Bty at Sherborne, P Bty at Blandford and Shaftesbury, Q Bty at Dorchester and Bridport, R Bty at Parkstone.

DORSET'S OWN YEOMANRY REGIMENT

A further TA reorganisation took place in 1961, when the 255th (WSY & DG) Medium Regt, RA, TA (formed by a previous merger of the West Somerset Yeomanry and the Dorset Garrison Artillery) was merged with the 294th to form the 250th QOD & WSY Medium Regt, RA, TA. However, the regiment only lasted 1967, when it was stood down at a further reorganisation of the TA. In 1994, 'Armour Replacement' was identified as being a role that could be undertaken by the TA, and subsequently it was decided to raise a new Yeomanry Regiment for this role and for it to be stationed at the RAC Centre, Bovington. During the next two and a half years planning took place and on 1st April 1997 it came to fruition and Dorset's own Yeomanry Regiment – 'The Dorset Yeomanry' – was raised, its *raison d'etre* being the need for an Armoured Delivery Group to oversee

25 pounder gun drill being demonstrated by the QODY Fd Bty, RA, during a fete at Bere Regis in about 1960.

tank replacement in operations like the Gulf War, its primary role thus being to deliver forward, crewed, combat ready, war maintenance reserve and replacement Armoured Fighting Vehicles (AFVs), to units that required replacements. In the 1999 TA reorganisation, the Dorset Yeomanry was reduced from three squadrons to one within the new Regiment, viz: A. (The Dorset Yeomanry) Armoured Replacement Squadron. The other three squadrons (formerly of the Royal Wessex

Men of A Squadron (The Dorset Yeomanry), of the Royal Wessex Yeomanry, instructing the Royal Marines in getting vehicles safely on and off landing craft at the Marines base at Hamworthy, Poole, in 2008 (Crown copyright).

The Regimental mascot, Lance Corporal Ramrod D'Arcy, a pure bred Dorset Horn Ram, who is looked after by the Ram Major.

Yeomanry) were B. (Royal Wiltshire Yeomanry), C. (Royal Gloucestershire Hussars) and D. (Royal Devon Yeomanry). Its uniform is based upon the previous QODY Dress – green the county colour being included and the Dorset Horned Ram's Head being adopted into the button design and for rank badges. In the Royal Wessex Yeomanry each squadron wears its own cap badge and mess kit, only the brown beret is now standard throughout, but the Dorset Yeomanry have a black diamond behind their badge to remind everyone of their association with the Royal Tank Regiment.

Regimental links have been cemented by the adoption of a pure bred Dorset Horn Ram as its mascot – Lance Corporal Ramrod D'Arcy being generously loaned by the Chairman of Young's Brewery, whilst the two principal Regimental Marches are Dorset tunes – 'Casterbridge' being the quick march and 'Sherborne' the slow march. The Dorset Yeomanry Squadron remains based at the Armour Centre, Bovington, as does RHQ, the Royal Wessex Yeomanry.

FIVE

BARRACKS, TENTED CAMPS, FORTS AND GUNSITES

Before proper barracks were built in the seventeenth and eighteenth centuries, troops, especially cavalry, were housed during the winter where they would best be able to get adequate stabling and forage.This usually meant splitting cavalry units down to individual troops. Such quartering was run by the constables or the local Justice of the Peace. Soldiers could not be billeted in private dwellings without the full approval of the residents, but rather, as records show they were put into 'inns, livery stables, ale-houses, victualling houses and all houses selling brandy, strong waters, cyder or metheglyn (a spiced mead) to be drunk on the premises.' Accommodation had to be paid for on departure and any officers who disregarded the law could be cashiered. Troops in such 'cavalry camps' were often used to help revenue officers in their attempts to prevent the smuggling then rife in the county.

In 1792, the post of Barrack Master General was created and numerous barracks were built all over England. By 1805, there were over 200 permanent or hired buildings that could accommodate some17,000 cavalry and 146,000 infantry, ready to repel any invasion. In Dorset there were permanent barracks in Dorchester, Bridport and Weymouth, also just across the Hampshire border at Christchurch (now in Dorset), to house cavalry and horse artillery. Those near the coast were well placed for anti-smuggling operations, doing away with the need for cavalry camps in places like Pimperne near Blandford Camp.

The Dorset Militia at camp at Playfields, now part of Poole, in 1877.

A Presentation being made to Mrs Bingham, wife of the then commander of the Dorset Militia, at Poundbury Barracks, June 1862, for her efforts to promote the welfare of the NCOs and men of the Regiment.

THE MILITIA & DEPOT BARRACKS

Suspended after the Napoleonic Wars, the Dorset Militia, together with the other county militias, was revived when, in 1851, Louis Napoleon Bonaparte staged a *coup d'état* and declared himself Emperor. In 1852, Dorset's militia quota was 506 men. A new colonel was appointed for Dorset (Col Bingham) and training was restarted in November 1852. However, they had no suitable place to store their equipment. Eventually, after much wrangling, the necessary money was raised to build a barracks (Marabout Barracks) that was completed in 1866, by a local contractor. At the far end of what used to be the old parade ground is a building comprising a central square tower with wings to the left and right. Called the 'Little Keep', it was once the entrance to the militia barracks and the Colonel's office and is all that remains of the old barracks. Behind it used to be a brick-built hospital with three wards, surgery and staff quarters.

Building standards were not high and more money had to be found for improvements (the magazine was underground, and thus permanently damp), so it was not until 1870 that the barracks could be occupied. However, the rooms always remained wet and needed fires burning continuously, so coal bills spiralled. The local authorities continually pressed the War Office to build a new Depot Barracks and to take the old Militia Barracks off their hands. In 1874 the War Office finally relented, choosing the site as the location for the new Depot Barracks for

The band of the Dorset Regiment playing outside the Keep in 1958, the year it amalgamated with the Devon Regiment.

the Dorsetshire Regiment.

The Depot Barracks, was completed in 1879 and built opposite the old barracks, with the splendid Keep as its gatehouse. The Keep was also used as both a guardhouse and the County Armoury (it now houses The Keep – Military Museum of Devon and Dorset). A comment at the time was that 'the barracks behind were

Blandford Camp in about 1910. The camp was started in the Boer War and though there were lines of primitve wooden huts many of those posted there found themselves bivouacked in tents. It was mainly used by the Yeomanry and other territorial units as a training camp for such skills as saddlery and marksmanship. In 1914 it became the base of the Royal Naval Division, and is now the home of the Royal Corps of Signals.

The troops mess-hall at Bovington Camp between the wars.

humble by comparison.' In these 'humble barracks', the Dorsets' Depot carried out its functions as an administrative centre. There was also a hospital there, plus a number of married quarters and a NAAFI Grocery shop. 'It was fun living in the barracks as a child,' wrote one young boy between the wars, 'there were lots of places to play . . . the boys played out imaginary wars . . . the girls played ball and skipping games in a grassy area near the schoolroom . . . They could bathe in the river from the lower slopes . . . and along Poundbury Road itself amongst a scrubby line of trees and bushes which we called Sherwood Forest.' There were of course places that were strictly off limits to children – stores and offices, the officers quarters or anywhere near 'The Square' (the Parade Ground).

BOVINGTON CAMP

In 1896 the War Office was looking for land in Dorset to use as a rifle and revolver range. They approached the Frampton family of Moreton and after some two years of protracted negotiations, on 16 February 1899, they agreed to pay £4,300 for just over 100 acres of heathland in the parishes of Bovington, Turners Puddle, Affpuddle and Wool to be used as a 'Rifle Range or for any other Military use or purpose.' Work soon began under the direction of a Royal Engineer officer from Weymouth in the building of a 1,000 yard long range with 20 butts. A caretaker was appointed – a Mr Woodrow of the Bryantspuddle brickyards (ex Dorsetshire Regiment). Accomodation was a tented camp some mile or so south of the range with a cottage for the caretaker.

On 4 June 1900, some 1,000 men of the 1st Bn. The Royal Southern Reserves became the first unit to move in for six weeks musketry firing, but the men of B

Bovington Camp just after the end of the Second World War. The AKC cinema in the centre was built by Italian POWs.

Company, 1st Volunteer Bn, Dorsetshire Regiment, who arrived about the same time, were the first unit to actually use the ranges. The caretaker's cottage was later let to the Purchase Brothers as a shop selling groceries, fizzy drinks and tobacco etc. Firewood for heating and cooking was bought from the Framptons, whilst Charles Cobb of Bere Regis first provided water with his horse-drawn tanker. As more was required a well was sunk and water pumped up by an oil-driven engine into large iron tanks (capacity, 3000 gallons). Soon two extra rooms were added to the Keeper's Cottage as a post office and canteen. It was also used as an officers' mess whilst one was being built and the Purchase Brothers became: 'Officers Mess caterers, general providers and tent kit suppliers'. The Territorials also used the range for their annual meeting of the Dorset Territorial Rifle Association. That apart, there was little social contact with the locals as there were few civilians in the area.

So many battalions living under canvas used the ranges in the decade before the First World War that the War Office had to enlarge the camp in 1907 and again in 1910, and they were to do so again when the war started.

WAACs at Bovington. Interior of the womens mess hut during the Second World War.

FORTS AND GUNSITES

1797 saw the first Corps of Artillery Volunteers being raised in Dorset, at Weymouth, Poole and Brownsea Island, which was the beginning of the Dorset Coastal Artillery. This was in step with Lord Milton's belief that any operational role should include giving early warning of a landing, providing guides for friendly troops, explaining any enemy advances and the driving of all livestock inland, while the Navy prevented enemy resupply or seawards evacuation. It was of course, never put to the test 'for real', although the Yeomanry did yearly exercises along these lines between May and October, apart from during haymaking or harvest. A stock recording system was evolved by Major Frampton and later adopted for all coastal districts in England. A few years later, John Penn, Governor of Portland, raised the first Volunteers on Portland, officially named the Royal Portland Legion (Coast Fencibles) (see *illustration on page 16*).

Later in the nineteenth century, engineers (and civilian contractors) built fortifications and gunsites to defend the new naval installations on Portland and to house the gun crews. There were various engineer units involved (eg: The Dorset Fortress and Electrical Regiment, RE), whose task was to equip the new fortifications, whilst the coastal artillery guns then had to be installed and manned by units such as the Dorset Coastal Artillery Regiment.

All these guns and supporting equipment are now mostly long gone, apart from those in museums such as the Museum of Coastal Defence at the Nothe Fort, Weymouth. Other forts, such as Blacknor and Upton, have been turned

A panoramic view of the Nothe Fort from the air.

Traction engines were used to haul heavy armaments up to Portland's forts. This 9.2 inch gun was bound for Blacknor Fort on West Cliff in 1909.

into private houses. Finally, there are still training camps in use such as Wyke Regis (RE bridging camp) and nearby Chickerell Camp. Whilst the forts and gun emplacements are already well described in Colin Pomeroy's 'Discover Dorset' *Castles & Forts*, perhaps a word or two here about the soldiers who built, and manned these gun emplacements would not go amiss. The RE were on Portland from about 1857, when plans were being finalised for the Victorian fortifications, the major feature being the Verne Citadel and its ancilliary gun batteries at East Wears. It became an infantry barracks in 1903, when its muzzle loading guns became obsolete with the change to breech loaders. Engineers remained there after the buildings were completed, for maintenance and new building work, right up to 1950 when it became a prison.

The men of the Coastal Artillery Regiment (who were Territorials after 1908) had initially occupied Red (also known as Weymouth) Barracks near the Nothe Fort, using the fort's guns for their regular practice firing, but moved to the Verne soon after the Second World War. The Verne could accommodate some 3,000 (normal military complement 1,000), allowing space for civilians in the event of an invasion. Coastal Regiment Gunners lived there and permanently manned the gun positions at East Wears right up to 1955. In 1961, the Regiment was merged with the QODY.

SIX

THE BOER WAR

Dorset played its part during the Boer War (1899-1902), with both infantry and cavalry Volunteers supporting the regular troops. After the 'Black Week' in December 1899, during which the British army suffered a series of heavy defeats at the hands of the Boers, the Government agreed to accept assistance from Volunteers, which they had previously declined, thus creating the Imperial Yeomanry. This would lead, for example, to the formation of a company of Yeomanry (the 26th 'Dorset' Company) as part of the 7th Battalion of the Imperial Yeomanry. At about the same time, an infantry company of Rifle Volunteers left Dorset, under Capt Kitson from Beaminster, to join the regular battalions of the Dorsets that were already serving at the front in South Africa. Among their Emblazoned Battle Honours were South African War (1899 – 1902) and the Relief of Ladysmith.

Volunteers from Wimborne bound for South Africa. They had volunteered for active service with the 1st Volunteer Battalion in 1900.

A decorative arch erected in South Street, Dorchester, to welcome home the 2nd Battalion from South Africa after they had disembarked at Southampton in October 1902.

THE DORSET RIFLE VOLUNTEERS

They were initially under strength but were soon joined by men from the Portland Volunteer Artillery. A number of farewell events were held, for example a Dorchester dinner at which some 290 gathered at the Corn Exchange in January 1900, whilst a few days later a dinner was held at Weymouth, and a Miss Ashley gave each volunteer a fitted writing case and a knife, fork and spoon set (again in a case). These were followed by Smoking Concerts (very popular in the Victorian era – usually musical evenings attended by men only!). Finally there were Farewell church services at which the Volunteers were given khaki-bound Bibles and the Freedom of the Borough. Most of those bound for South Africa also had their lives insured for £100 (paid for by friends, to be given to their surviving relatives should they fail to return).

The Company (91 strong) left Dorchester on 3 April and sailed the same day from the Albert Docks. They landed in Durban in early May and later helped General Buller clear the Boers from northern Natal. They took part in fierce engagements at Botha's Pass and Almond's Nek where the Dorsets carried the rocky hilltop at bayonet point with the assistance of the Volunteer Company. Later, after more heavy fighting, they spent several months at Van Reenan's Pass digging earthworks before embarking for home. Capt Kitson was Mentioned in Despatches and two Volunteers were awarded DCMs, whilst six men remained in South Africa to join

Presentations took place throughout Dorset after the return of the troops from South Africa in 1902. The photograph above is of watches being presented outside Shaftesbury Town Hall, the one below of medals being presented at the Dorchester Depot to men of the 2nd Battalion.

the Johannesburg Police or to be invalided home.

The Western Gazette of 14th June reported that at about 8pm the evening before, the train carrying the returning Volunteers 'approached the L and SW Railway Station at Dorchester, when a salvo of fog signals was fired and a loud cheer raised. Officers of the Depot and the Weymouth, Bridport and Artillery

Broadwindsor welcomes home Tommy Ackerman on his return from South Africa.

Volunteers were there to welcome them. The Company was joined by those already invalided home . . . The cheers increased to a crescendo as they marched down Weymouth Avenue and South Street. The Volunteers showed evident pleasure as they recognised relatives and friends in the crowd. Flags fluttered everywhere. At the entrance to South Street a triumphal arch was erected . . . the men were absolutely besieged and they must have shaken hands until their arms ached.'

THE 26TH (DORSET) COMPANY, 7TH BATTALION
THE IMPERIAL YEOMANRY

On 1st January 1900, Lord Ilchester, Lord Lieutenant of Dorset called a county meeting at Dorchester, at which over £4,000 was subscribed towards a total of £9,635 needed to equip the Dorset Company. Within eight days, the permitted establishment had been exceeded and two months later, in March 1900, the Company, all of whom had volunteered for one year's overseas service, landed at Table Bay. They first came under fire just 15 weeks after Lord Ilchester's meeting, taking part in numerous operations whilst acting as part of the advance guard of Lord Roberts' army. They were the first troops into Pretoria, but then had to withdraw, so that Lord Roberts could make a triumphal entry the following day!

After the capture of Pretoria, they were involved in chasing the elusive Boer General de Wit. When they were finally ordered home in 1902, 281 Dorset Yeomen had served in South Africa, three had been killed in action, six died of fever and one of pleurisy and 16 were wounded. The Order of the Bath was awarded to the CO, Col Browne, the DSO to Capt Sir Elliott Leese and the DCM to Sgt Bragge, nine of the company were Mentioned in Despatches and ten Other Ranks had been commissioned from the ranks.

SEVEN

THE FIRST WORLD WAR

BOVINGTON, WORGRET AND LULWORTH
AND A FLOOD OF VOLUNTEERS

There was no conscription in Britain in 1914, but her small, highly trained Expeditionary Force of 150,000 men (six divisions) could be speedily mobilised. Lord Kitchener, Minister for War, knew he would need more volunteers and hoped to recruit some 100,000 in the first six months and perhaps half a million altogether. However, he had not reckoned on the wave of patriotic fervour that was to sweep the country – half a million volunteered in the first month alone!

In Dorset, in the first month, 2,258 volunteers reported to the Depot barracks in Dorchester and were sent to Worgret Camp near Wareham. The flood of volunteers caused chaos in the Army – there were shortages of uniforms, weapons and accommodation. Every available camp was brought into service – Bovington became the initial training camp for the newly-formed 17th Infantry Division – composed mainly of men from the north – Yorkshire, Lancashire and Northumberland for example, although the 6th Dorsets were part of its 50th Brigade. They certainly did not appreciate their arrival in 'sunny Dorset', one Lancashire lad writing home that they had 'spent the first night on the verge

Worgret Camp near Wareham was where most volunteers in Dorset were sent to for initial training. This photograph is of an Army Service Corps Field Bakery at the Camp in 1915.

Mustering horses for the army at Broadwindsor on August 5th 1914, nine days after the start of the First World War. Over 2 million horses were killed during the course of the war.

The outbreak of the war led to many marriages, as here between Bert Chaffey and Edith Mitchener in Poole. We can't be certain, but it seems probable that Bert survived the war.

By early 1915 Blandford was almost a garrison town, so crowded was it with troops from various regiments, as well as the Yeomanry and Royal Naval Division.

of the road, no tents or rations having arrived.' The local paper headlines read: 'Kitchener's Army stranded with no food or covering.'

The division's three brigades were eventually sent to three different camps – the 50th to Worgret, the 51st to Lulworth and the 52nd to Bovington. The first uniforms were issued towards the end of September, but they were not new – just thin and patched re-issues, whilst the first consignment of rifles were outdated Lee Enfields and Lee Metfords. It was not until the following March that more modern equipment arrived, and the Division was not fully equipped until they were on the point of leaving for France in the autumn of 1915.

As elsewhere in Dorset, 'Tea and Rest Rooms' were set up in the Dorchester Corn Exchange.

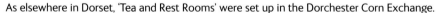

The Call Up for reserves outside Blandford Corn Exchange in 1915.

On 13 September four trains, containing 4,000 recruits from Manchester and Stockport, arrived at Wool Station and marched the two miles to Bovington. Gradually the camp became better organised and even the weather improved. Squads of soldiers could be seen doing drill, PT etc and playing football in their spare time. The YMCA did yeoman service, serving refreshments and providing a writing room. However, accommodation was still at a premium and, as the weather worsened with the onset of winter, the authorities rashly promised to house the tented soldiers in wooden huts. Despite employing every local carpenter in the entire area and even with help from the troops, it was obvious that this was a promise that could not be met, so it was decided to put troops into civilian billets until the huts were ready.

On the last day of November 1914, the troops marched off in all directions – Wimborne, Canford, Broadstone, Ferndown and Kinson, to name but a few of their destinations. They only expected to be billeted for about eight weeks, but it would be four months before the huts were ready. Bovington Camp then comprised eight sets of lines, lettered from A to H, each set being occupied by a battalion. Each hut accommodated 30 men. There were also more wooden huts as offices, guardrooms, canteens, churches, cookhouses etc, whilst a large hospital block was built to the south of A,B and C lines.

Arrival of the tanks in Dorset. Part of the Tank Park at Bovington Camp in 1916.

17TH DIVISION DEPART

Having completed their training the 17th departed and their place was taken by the 7th Reserve Battalion of the Dorsetshire Regiment whose role was to train local volunteers as reserves for the battalions in France. When they were disbanded in 1916, the Australian Army began using Bovington as a place for toughening up wounded soldiers, after being discharged from hospital and before returning to their units. The horrors of the Somme soon had Bovington overflowing again and so Worgret was also used by the Australians. However, a major change of permanent 'resident' was soon on its way – the tanks were coming.

ARRIVAL OF THE TANKS

The First World War would change Dorset in numerous ways, one of the most important being the invention of a revolutionary weapon of war whose arrival in the county brought about vast changes, especially to the hitherto untouched heathland in the south. This was of course the tank, which it was hoped would end the stalemate on the Western Front that had been brought about by the plethora of opposing trench systems, barbed wire entanglements, machine guns and artillery which had virtually stopped movement. The tank's basic characteristics were firepower, protection and mobility – all of which were a complete contrast to the static trench warfare that had all but brought the war to a halt whilst increasing the casualties.

Men of the Local Defence Volunteers initially had to make do without uniforms and being armed with wooden rifles when first formed early in the war, but by 1916 they had been organised into proper battalions . Seventeen detachments were raised in Dorset. These men were members of the Sherborne detachment in 1917.

Prisoner of War camps were established at Blandford and Dorchester. The one at Dorchester was in the area below Poundbury, and up to 3,000 Germans were housed there. They were set to work laying electricity cables in the town and doing general manual labour. I presume the rabbits were being bred to eat.

Early tank training on the Bovington Training Area. The tank may have brought about a revolutionary change in the tactics of warfare, but boggy ground remained as much an obstacle as ever.

Tanks were first built in Lincoln in 1915, and first properly tested on Lord Iveagh's estate at Elveden in Norfolk. However, it soon became clear that this area was too small for training the large numbers of tank crews that were going to be needed, and it was decided to switch to Bovington in Dorset. The story of how Bovington and Lulworth camps grew into the size they are today will be told later, but when the first tanks began to arrive they were accompanied by tight security, with guards who were armed with rifles and bayonets and had orders to shoot trespassers.

In mid-1916, under great secrecy, the complete establishment of the Heavy Section moved from Elveden to Bovington – a motley crew by all accounts with hardly two uniforms alike – kilts, breeches, trousers, leggings, puttees and field boots; buttons of brass, silver gilt, leather and bone were all to be seen. They trained for hours on end, carrying their kit, in single file, at the double until they dropped from exhaustion. Those who did were sent to other units and those who had the stamina became members of the Machine-Gun Corps, Heavy Section.

One volunteer recalled: 'It was a bitterly cold day in November 1916, when, with about 40 others, I arrived at Bovington Camp. We were all ASC men and had been transferred into the new branch of the Army then styled the Tank Corps. We had left comfortable billets at Osterley Park in London for the wilds of Dorset and I must say we were by no means impressed. Bovington in those far off days was a dreary spot indeed and the wintry weather (snow was falling when we reached Wool) did not help to cheer us. On arriving at Wool, we dumped our kitbags at the station and marched the half-mile or so to the camp.'

LULWORTH CAMP

Lulworth has been the home of the Tank Gunnery School since 1916, when it first became necessary to find a suitable area to practice tank gunnery away from prying eyes. The camp was initially completely tented, which proved chaotic in the south-westerly gales that swept up Bindon Valley, blowing tents and their belongings, hundreds of yards away. They would have disappeared altogether had it not been for a strategically planted barrier of trees at the north-east edge of the camp. Very gradually they were replaced by huts, but Lulworth always lagged behind Bovington when it came to improving facilities.

GROWTH IN BOVINGTON

Towards the end of 1917, the Heavy Section became the Tank Corps and expanded from nine to eighteen battalions, so the Tank Training Centre at Bovington also increased in size – there were now over 300 training tanks in Bovington alone (it would reach nearly 600 before the end of the war), and an ever-increasing requirement arose for adequate repair facilities. These began as canvas shelters, but soon permanent galvanised iron steel framed buildings, 50 feet by 35 feet, with concrete floors and overhead cranes were erected. Additionally, there was a smithy, a foundry, a coppersmith's shop, an acetylene welding shop and a new machine shop. There was now clearly a need for far more electricity than the camp generating system could produce, and it became necessary to build first one, than a second, generating station (run by the Royal Engineers).

The camp administrative staff also grew and now included a number of WAACs (Women's Army Auxiliary Corps) who acted as cooks and waitresses, etc in the many messes and cookhouses of the camp. The heathland near the camp became dotted with networks of practice trenches, whilst a narrow, 18 gauge light rail track was laid to make the transportation of stores and vehicle spares easier.

In the autumn of 1918, it was decided to double the size of the Tank Corps, which meant raising eighteen new battalions at Bovington and spending some £500,000 on new technical buildings. Work began immmediately and by early November half the programme had been completed. However, the Armistice was signed on 11 November and the War Office cancelled all further tank production.

EIGHT

THE DORSETSHIRE REGIMENT
1914 – 1918

Prior to the First World War, both the 1st and 2nd Battalions of the Dorsetshire Regiment had served in India and South Africa (Boer War), then, when war began, ten 'Hostilities Only' battalions were formed. Of the resulting dozen, six would serve overseas, the 1st, 5th and 6th in Europe on the Western Front, the remainder in the Middle East. The 2nd Battalion was in Poona when the war began and was shipped to the Persian Gulf, arriving in early November, then advancing and taking Basra, despite suffering some 170 casualties. Further battles followed, such as Ahwaz - against a mass of Arab cavalry – and Shaiba, where a charge by the Dorsets across 200 yards of open ground put the Turks to flight.

The force reached Kut in April 1915, only to be trapped there, then taken prisoner a year later after an horrific siege and final surrender. Only 70 men of the remaining 350 Dorsets would subsequently survive the brutal captivity that followed. During the siege, the returning sick and wounded from hospital, plus the few replacement personnel that were sent out but obviously could not join the battalion, they were linked up with similar drafts bound for the 2nd Battalion The Norfolks to form an ad hoc battalion which became part of the forces attempting

Conscripts for the 5th Battalion are inspected at Dorchester in early August 1914. As a result of Kitchener's finger pointing from posters on hoardings throughout the county – 'Your Country Needs YOU' – new recruits flooded in, the vast majority being Dorset born and bred.

"Kut Fund" Day

IN DORCHESTER
Wednesday, July 26th, 1916.

NOT a Celebration of VICTORY, but a Celebration of Splendid
VALOUR in a great and all but impossible enterprise, and a
COMBINED EFFORT TO SEND SUCCOUR
to Very Gallant Men,

370 DORSET SOLDIERS

who capitulated to FAMINE, not to the FOE, in closely-beleaguered
Kut-el-Amara with General Townshend's Army, April 28th, 1916.

Particulars of Procession
OF
Troops and Decorated Cars

Representing the
ARMY AND NAVY, OUR DOMINIONS, CROWN COLONIES, AND
DEPENDENCIES, OUR STAUNCH AND GALLANT ALLIES,
WITH MISCELLANEOUS FEATURES.

To show in a practical manner Dorset's appreciation of its County
Regiments, whose Heroic Achievements and Endurance have added
to their splendid record, won them imperishable Fame, and
earned the everlasting admiration and gratitude of their fellow
countrymen. Loosen your Purse Strings and show your patriotism,
in a manner worthy of Dorset by providing an abundance of funds
for the assistance of those held Prisoners of War.

The Procession will be formed in the Square of the Dorset Depot Barracks at 1 p.m.
Marshalled by Mr. Councillor Benjamin Carruthers, and thence start at 1-30 p.m. to
Parade the principal Streets and Roads of the Borough.
ROUTE OF PROCESSION.
High West Street, South Street, South Walks, South Walks Road,
High Street, Fordington, High East Street, South Street, Great
Western Road, Cornwall Road

'Kut Day' 1916 in Dorchester.
A fundraising day was held in
Weymouth and Bridport as well,
and some £1,600 was raised
to provide comforts for the
survivors of the 2nd Battalion
after their surrender at Kut at
the hands of the Turks.

Men of the 1st Battalion halt on August 31st 1914 during the retreat from Mons.

to relieve Kut. It was known officially as the 'Composite English Battalion', but also nicknamed 'The 'Norsets'! This battalion was broken up when the 2nd Dorsets was reformed. Of the remaining battalions to serve overseas, the 1st /4th served in India and Mesopotamia, the 1st /5th in India, Egypt and Palestine, whilst the 5th Battalion landed at Gallipoli, then served in Egypt and Palestine, but would finish the war on the Western Front.

The 1st Battalion, as part of the BEF, sailed for France on 14 August 1914, and were in action just nine days later at Mons. After fighting bravely among the slagheaps, they withdrew in good order the 150 miles back to the Marne. It was blisteringly hot and the roads were clogged with stragglers. Nevertheless they recrossed the Aisne and dug in with, as Hugh Popham recounts in his history of the regiment, *The Dorset Regiment*, 'the river at their backs and a dauntingly superior enemy force in front'.

The Germans then made for the Channel whilst the BEF was transferred to Flanders. At La Bassee that October the 1st Battalion suffered over 50 casualties, then at Pont Fixe the following day a further 335 casualties, the remainder earning praise from Lord French who spoke of the 'fine fighting of the Dorsets'. Worse was to come at Hill 60, where the Germans attacked with poison gas. This was not the first gas attack, but the German trenches were so close that the British could see the nozzles that were discharging the chlorine gas. To escape the fumes the men dropped to the bottom of their trenches, where unfortunately the gas (being heavier than air) collected in a every hollow – forming a deadly concentration. Fortunately one officer realised what was happening and ordered his men to climb up to the parapets where they were relatively safe, and then ordered them to fire into the poisonous clouds. The attack failed mainly because the wind changed and some of the gas drifted back over the German lines. However, the enemy tried again a few days later with more success and the Dorsets lost over 170 men, including their CO. They would lose many more that week and finally the Hill as well.

By the end of 1914 the Dorset's had seen action at Mons and in the first battle of Ypres, leading to the first casualties arriving at the Military Hospital in Dorchester Barracks.

Meanwhile the newly raised 5th Battalion landed at Sulva Bay in an attempt to resolve the impasse at Gallipoli. This allowed the Turks time to reinforce and prevent the Dorset's from taking the vital high ground. The battalion's progress came to a halt, the stalemate unresolved. This parlous situation remained unchanged throughout 1916 and 1917 with the 1st, 5th and 6th, as Popham comments, being 'swallowed up in the mighty military machine on the Western Front, whose numbers rose . . . to 1,343,000 when the 5th arrived.' Conditions were appalling, with mud waist-high, trench foot and widespread scurvy, as was pneumonia and fever.

The 1st Battalion in February 1915 in a trench on the Western Front.

Above Writing home from the trenches. Men of C Company, the 1st Battalion writing letters home in January 1915 from a fire trench in western Flanders.

Below The tragedy of the First World War is perfectly summed up in this photograph from the Dorset County Museum. On it is written 'Trevett & Papa, killed in the Great War'.

Equally appalling was the fate of the 2nd Battalion, encircled at Kut, with surrender inevitable, some 1,200 of the garrison's sick, were permitted to leave in an exchange of prisoners, whilst the remainder, as already mentioned, were marched a thousand miles into Anatolia – only a handful surviving the horrendous journey.

On the Western Front, the final German offensive of the war began in March 1918, but fortunately was unsuccessful, the British divisions, including the Dorsets, stubbornly contesting every foot of ground and losing some 250 men in the fighting – 'haggard, dead tired, depleted; but never broken' is how the battalion's history describes this

A long overdue memorial to the Dorsetshire Regiment was unveiled in France in May 2011 in honour of the 4,060 men of the Regiment killed in action during the First World War. Appropriately, it stands on the start line for the first day of the Battle of the Somme, 1 July 1916, a day on which 350 soldiers from the Regiment were killed. Bugle Major Cox played the last post and reveille on a silver bugle presented to the Dorsetshire Regiment in 1920. The 8 foot high memorial was carved by sculptors Zoe Cull and Alex Evans at their Bockhampton workshop, and bears the regimental crest and a quotation from Thomas Hardy: 'Victory crowns the just'.

retreat. However, by the summer, German progress was halted – not the least by the arrival of the Americans, who restored movement to the battle, so the Dorsets, despite initially suffering heavy casualties whilst crossing the Ancre, made steady progress. The assault on the Hindenburg line followed in mid-September, the morale and offensive spirit never faltering despite the conditions as the 'War to end all wars' ground to a close.

The regimental historian wrote of their war record 'It is customary to raise monuments to the dead and, very rightly to inscribe thereon the names of those who made the supreme sacrifice; but the Dorsets' Roll of Honour is the Regimental Roll. For a regiment that had had its full share of death and glory and was awarded 48 battle honours ranging from Shaiba to the Somme, it provides a just and generous epigraph.'

NINE

BETWEEN THE WARS

THE TANK CORPS CENTRE

As we have seen, the Tank Corps was now well established in Dorset, despite having been greatly reduced in numbers at the end of the First World War. The Central Schools at Bovington and Lulworth had had their share of reductions, in 1919, for example, they had comprised an HQ and the following Schools: Machine Gun, Tank, Signalling, Intelligence, Compass, Revolver, Anti-Gas, Bombing and Pigeon (Message Carrying). By 1922 they had been cut down/merged and all that remained were Headquarters, Gunnery School, Tank Driving and Maintenance School and Armoured Car School. The Tank Driving School had two branches at Bovington and Wareham. The number of instructors was also greatly reduced as rapid demobilisation took its toll. Obsolete tanks were disposed of (mostly by the Slough Trading Company) and newer ones obtained for instructional purposes.

The major task of the Schools became the training of unit instructors, whilst at Worgret Camp a mile west of Wareham, the 1st (Depot) Tank Battalion was formed in 1919, moving to Bovington two years later to occupy F, G, and H Lines, thereafter known as 'The Eighth of August Lines' (so named to commemorate the Germans 'Black Day' which had begun their slide to final defeat, the '100

2nd Battalion of the Dorsets receive their war medals at Portland on 28 July 1919.

47

One of the Royal Tank Corps most famous recruits, Colonel T. E. Lawrence, universally known as 'Lawrence of Arabia' and who joined the RTC in March 1923, as a private soldier, using the name T. E. Shaw. Tragically, in 1935, whilst living in his cottage at Clouds Hill, he was knocked off his motorcycle, dying of his injuries in the Bovington Medical Centre. His grave is at Moreton, his cottage now belongs to the National Trust, and there is a magnificent effigy of him in Arab dress, carved by Eric Kennington, in St Martin's Church, Wareham.

Days Battle' ending with the Armistice on 11th November 1918). In 1925,the 1st (Depot) Battalion became the Royal Tank Corps Depot (the Tank Corps having become 'Royal' on 18 October 1923).

The Beret Arrives and a Famous Recruit

Army Council Instruction No 113 of 1925 stated that a black beret with a white metal badge (silver for officers) in substitution of the Service Dress Cap was to be worn in all orders of dress by the RTC – a very sensible item of dress to wear inside the confines of an armoured fighting vehicle. However, it certainly raised comment in the press.

Two years earlier, in March 1923, under the alias of T. E. Shaw, one of Britain's most famous soldiers, namely Colonel T. E. Lawrence, after being hounded out of the RAF by the press, had enlisted as a private soldier in the Tank Corps at Bovington and was posted to 'B' Coy, Depot Bn, being allocated a bed in Hut 12. He made two firm friends during his brief sojourn in the Corps – Privates Russell and Palmer, who were both quiet men who read and listened to music. Whilst at Bovington he rented from a relative a small almost derelict cottage a mile from Bovington called Clouds Hill, for the princely sum of two shillings and sixpence a week. Sergeant Knowles, who had a neighbouring cottage, helped him renovate it and, whenever he could, Lawrence would escape to this peaceful refuge to read, write or listen to his records, either alone or with friends. After two years in the Tank Corps, getting steadily more depressed – almost suicidal at one point – influential friends began a campaign to get him back into the RAF and eventually,

HM King George V during a visit to Lulworth in April 1928.

in 1925, he was readmitted. Lawrence then spent a relatively enjoyable ten years, incognito, until in 1935, when, as Aircaftsman Shaw, he left the Services, returning to Clouds Hill to write. However, he was once again besieged by reporters, eager to know what the great 'Lawrence of Arabia' was going to do next. Sadly before he could decide, he was critically injured in a motorcycle accident in 1935, just two weeks after returning to Dorset, when he swerved to avoid a young cyclist near his cottage at Clouds Hill. He was taken to the Bovington Camp Medical Centre but died six days later. His grave in Moreton churchyard is now, like Clouds Hill, a popular tourist attraction. On 13 May 1983, Tom Beaumont, who had been Lawrence's armoured car driver in Arabia, planted a tree close to the spot where Lawrence had crashed 48 years earlier. A plaque at the base of the tree reads: 'Near this spot Lawrence of Arabia crashed his motor cycle and was fatally injured, 13 May 1935.'

Camp Followers

The size of Bovington – or 'Tin Town' as it was now called locally – gradually increased as a number of traders sensing the obvious needs of the soldiers and their families moved in. They erected a variety of wooden huts, tin shacks and even old railway carriages, on the southern edge of the camp. Railway carriages could be bought for £20 (plus a £20 delivery charge), one of the strangest uses being to house a piano belonging to a music teacher who gave lessons from hers. By the early 1920s there were barbers, cobblers, chemists, tailors, grocers,

Royal Engineers posing for the photographer whilst bridge-building on the River Stour between the wars.

blacksmiths and butchers, as well as five cafes, two billiard saloons, two bicycle shops, a fish and chip parlour, garage and laundry. 'Tin Town' soon rivalled nearby Wareham in size and complexity!

BLANDFORD

Bovington and Lulworth were not the only places to change between the wars. The camp near Blandford, which had been used by the Royal Navy during the war, reverted to farming use when the units were disbanded and the wooden huts sold off to local villagers. The land was then used for grazing or reverted to scrub. However, Blandford continued to support the Territorial Army, and in May 1922, the 94th (Dorset & Somerset) Field Brigade RA, TA, was formed, consisting of two batteries of the former Somerset RHA TA and two squadrons of the Queens Own Dorset Yeomanry, that were converted to 375 and 376 Field Batteries, stationed at Blandford, Shaftesbury and Sherborne. Further re-organisation took place in 1928 and 1937.

During the months of tension leading up to the Second World War, Blandford Camp was once again chosen as a place to concentrate the military and in July 1939, a tented camp was erected and manned by a cadre of regular officers and NCOs. Young men, straight from civilian life, began arriving for training in drill, PT, marching and basic weapon training. The camp soon comprised some 100 marquees and over 490 smaller tents. Next a wooden hutted camp was built in 1939-40, in 'Lines' that became known as 'Spiders'. Basic training was still given, but also part of the camp was occupied by an RA, AA regiment to train those who would become Ack Ack (anti-aircraft) Gunners. This continued during early 1940, as troops were concentrated in the south and south-east, in case of possible invasion threats following Dunkirk. Blandford quickly became a massive transit camp for troops evacuated from France, in particular men from the 3rd Division.

TEN

THE SECOND WORLD WAR

PHONEY WAR AND THE THREAT OF INVASION
1939-1941

The BEF goes to France

It had been agreed before the war began that Britain's main contribution to any war effort would be restricted to naval and air activity so as to avoid having to send an expeditionary force to the Continent. However, this agreement was changed even before the war began and Britain agreed to send a sizeable expeditionary force, together with an air component. By the time war was declared this had grown to over 160,000 men, all of whom would be transported to France without a single casualty. Within one of the three BEF Corps was Major General Montgomery's 3rd Infantry Division, which had prepared itself for embarkation in a concentration area in Dorset and Somerset. HM The King visited the 'Iron' Division as it had been known since the First World War, whilst it was in Dorset. Other units of the

HM King George VI visiting an AA gunsite in Dorset in the early days of the war.

Exercising one of the 9.2 inch guns at Blacknor Fort on Portland.

BEF temporarily stationed in Dorset included the Royal West Kents, the Durham Light Infantry and the Black Watch. The Nothe Fort was operational with its main armament being three breech-loading 6in guns and two 6pdr QF guns in the coastal defence role, whilst AA defence was provided by a battery of 3.7in AA guns. Some of these, in particular the AA guns, saw regular action and on one occasion in July 1940, the 6in guns opened fire 'across the bows' of two unidentified ships in Weymouth Bay. Fortunately they were swiftly identified as friendly vessels, carrying refugees from the Channel Islands.

Blitzkrieg!

Following the quiet period known as the 'Phoney War', Germany unleashed its 'Blitzkrieg' on France and the Low Countries on 10 May 1940. In a few short weeks, the BEF was forced back to the coast and was in grave danger of being annihilated – saved only by the 'Miracle of Dunkirk'. In total some 338,000 men were taken off the beaches between 29 May and 4 June, when Dunkirk finally fell. Britain now stood alone against the Nazis and a German invasion appeared to be inevitable. Hasty plans were made to defend the entire south coast of England, including Dorset.

Local Defence Volunteers/Home Guard

On 14 May 1940, Secretary of State for War, Anthony Eden, broadcast an appeal for men to join the Local Defence Volunteers. Thousands responded immediately, despite a shortage of weapons, equipment and uniforms. The LDV would later blossom into the well-equipped Home Guard, which even contained a secret guerrilla force, highly trained to cause maximum disruption to any invading enemy.

Piddletrenthide Home Guard Company's mounted section.

Coastal Defences and Anti-aircraft Guns

The 2nd Bn Lincolnshire Regiment was the main army garrison on Portland, based at the Verne Citadel. There were coastal defence artillery batteries at East Weares Point and Blacknor Headland, manned by the Portland Coast Artillery Garrison, which was the Dorsetshire Heavy Regiment, RA, TA. Light AA defences were provided by 75th LAA Bty, RA, another TA unit mainly recruited from Weymouth, Poole and Portland. Eventually they would get 40mm Bofors, but initially they had to make do with old First World War Lewis guns. Over in the east of the county in Christchurch (then in Hampshire), the 9th Medium Regiment, RA, occupied the old

The Prime Minister, Winston Churchill, watches a Universal Bren Gun Carrier on the road near Wareham in July 1940 (IWM H 2277).

A Heavy Ack Ack Site at Holton Heath to protect the Royal Naval Cordite Factory.

horse artillery barracks. The artillery connection would continue in 1943-44 when the Canadian 14th Field Regiment were billeted there and in the town. However, the most well-known military unit in Christchurch was the Royal Engineers Experimental Bridging Establishment, one of whose civilian designers would be knighted for inventing the Bailey Bridge.

In addition to the coastal batteries already mentioned, there were others being set up all along the Dorset coast, from Lyme Regis in the west (2 x 4.7in guns), to Hengistbury Head (2 x 4in) in the east, including: Abbotsbury (2 x 4in), West Bay (2 x 5.5in), Swanage (2 x 4in), Brownsea Island (2 x 4.7in), and even some ex 1909 vintage 6in field guns at Branksome in open positions. At West Bay, the area had been effectively sealed off and those inhabitants who hadn't been evacuated, needed passes to enter the village. The houses on West Cliff had become billets for the garrison who had been told to 'fight to the last round and the last man.'

Heavy Ack Ack Sites

Initially there were just eight in total – four around Weymouth and four at Holton Heath (to protect the Royal Naval Cordite Factory). They were equipped with a mixture of old 3in and 3.7in AA guns. The Light AA were no better armed, old Lewis guns being their main armament. However, things did improve and by 1941, there were over 80 LAA gunsites on the coast between Lulworth and Hengistbury Head and similar numbers to the west, some even on the tops of high buildings in coastal towns like Poole and Bournemouth.

Motor Cycle Reconnaissance Troops of the Northumberland Fusiliers at Blandford Camp shortly after being reformed in the wake of Dunkirk.

Searchlight Detachments

The 2nd Searchlight Regiment, RA, was the unit providing this other vital component of AA defence in Dorset and Hampshire, with its HQ and Training School, both at Cranborne. The regiment had been reformed after Dunkirk with men who had survived from the two searchlight regiments. They were later made up to full strength with 475 Bty of the 82nd Searchlight Regiment that had been stationed in the Portland/Weymouth area.

Gun Operations Room (GOR)

In 1939, a skeleton GOR was set up in the Red Barracks at the Nothe Fort at Weymouth, to co-ordinate all AA defences in Dorset. It moved to bigger and better equipped quarters in early 1940, still in the Red Barracks and stayed there until late 1941, when it was relocated at Nottington House, just off the Dorchester road outside Weymouth.

All this time it had been known as the 'Portland GOR' as it controlled the Portland guns. Then in 1941, a second GOR was set up for the guns in East Dorset, in particular the ones protecting the cordite factory. This GOR was located at South Lytchett Manor. It was manned by a mixture of RA and R Signals personnel, including ATS.

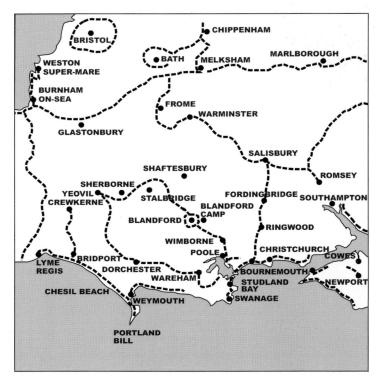

Map showing the principal Southern Command stop lines in Dorset and the surrounding area. Note the concentration round Blandford, which because of its camps was intended to be a major obstacle to any German inland advance.

Defensive Stop Lines in the West Country

With a German invasion expected at any time, hasty plans were made to protect the coastline with concrete pillboxes, tank obstacles on the beaches and across the most vulnerable approaches from the sea inland. Minefields were laid on the beaches and barbed wire entanglements were erected everywhere. The piers at Bournemouth and Boscombe were gapped. Even some of the old tanks from the Tank Museum were used as roadblocks, whilst stakes were driven into open fields to prevent airborne troops from landing. Inland from the coast a series of stop lines were constructed with pillboxes, tank traps, etc to obstruct, channel and contain enemy thrusts that had broken through the beach defences. As well as these static obstacles, mobile columns were organised in both Bovington and Lulworth camps, comprising a light tank troop, a medium tank troop, two motorised troops, and a reserve troop, all under command of a column HQ. Known as BOVCOL and LULCOL, the columns had the ability to move swiftly and at short notice anywhere in a 45mile radius of the camps.

A prewar Vickers medium tank is used to bolster the defences (barbed wire and 'dragons teeth') at Arish Mell Gap.

The Green Howards on coastal defence at Studland. One of the units in 60th Bde, 50th Division who fought with the BEF in France, enjoying a cup of tea.

'Project Fougasse'. The Sea Flame barrage of burning oil being ignited during trials at Studland in 1941 (IWM H 7020).

Fort Henry and Studland Beach Defences

The last of the fortlike structures to be built in the county was 'Fort Henry' at Redend Point on the southern end of Studland Bay. Built by Canadian engineers in 1944, this blockhouse was designed and built as a safe place for VIPs (such as Churchill, Eisenhower and Montgomery) to watch the mock invasion exercises that took place in Studland Bay in 1944.

Probably the strangest beach defences to be tried out in Studland Bay was a system of underwater pipes used to release a series of oilslicks that could then be ignited to destroy enemy landing parties. Known as 'Project Fougasse', it was trialled on three occasions during the winter of 1940/41 and it was said the light produced was so bright that you could read a newspaper in the middle of Bournemouth. Shortage of suitable steel piping, however, restricted its use on a wide scale.

STANDING ALONE
1942 – 1943

By 1941, the immediate threat of invasion by the Nazis had lessened, but Britain still 'stood alone' apart from the unfailing support of the Commonwealth. 1942 was in the words of Prime Minister Churchill ' a year of toil – a year of struggle and peril and a long step forward to victory'. In Dorset, there had been air-raids from 1940 onwards and many places in the county had been bombed, but nowhere heavier than the naval base at Portland. Nevertheless, it was not all one sided, the AA defences shooting down a number of German aircraft, a typical action over Bournemouth, for example, resulting in two enemy aircraft being shot down,

A Civil Defence Gas Decontamination Squad on exercise outside the entrance to Dorchester Prison in North Square, April 1941.

one by a triple mounted Lewis gun. The two Lance Bombardiers who manned it were awarded the BEM for this action and for rescuing both their comrades and guns, carrying them down Beales department store's spiral staircase. Elsewhere members of Royal Engineer Bomb Disposal squads defused unexploded bombs, whilst Royal Marine commandos were trained in a large amphibious warfare centre near Hamworthy. And of course the Home Guard had lost its 'Dad's Army' image and become a force to be reckoned with, countrywide numbering between one and a half and two million men. In Dorset, from about September 1941, Home Guard units were trained to operate coast artillery and AA defences, thus releasing regular troops for other duties. Post-war, Harry Fox of Lulworth had this to say about his local unit: 'They were a fine, brave, determined and stubborn lot of fellows, the core being First World War veterans, who had been through the mill and knew what to expect if the enemy ever reached us. They were not the fools many youngsters of today picture them to be and many sported quite an array of medal ribbons.'

A Bomb Disposal Team after successfuly defusing a 1,000lb unexploded bomb after a severe raid on Weymouth in which the hospital was badly damaged. It took the Team five days to bring the bomb to the surface and deal with it.

59

The Home Guard. No 3 Platoon, A Coy, 4th (Sherborne) Bn photographed in 1943. The curious weapon at the front is a Spigot Mortar (known as The Blacker Bombard) that could fire a 14 lb bomb some 800 yards.

An Armed Camp

The south of England slowly became one gigantic armed camp as the months passed. Nowhere was more intimately concerned with the coming invasion of occupied Europe than the beautiful and deceptively peaceful county of Dorset. The Americans were yet to arrive, but in addition to the British troops, ships and planes, there were many important civilian establishments, some highly secret, buried in Dorset's quiet lanes and sleepy villages. Various members of the Special Operations Executive (SOE) for example, arrived in Poole in late 1941 to form the Small Scale Raiding Force, with the aim of carrying out raids across the Channel. Anderson Manor, near Winterborne Zelston was chosen as its headquarters. At Lyme Regis units included a Royal Signals Pigeon Section which set up seven lofts, sending many birds to secret agents in occupied France. Early in the war, Bournemouth was nominated a 'Defence Area' which meant that civilian visitors to the town were banned, civilian movement restricted and many hotels requisitioned for Government use. Nearly every hotel played its part during the war and some hosted such VIPs as Generals Eisenhower and Montgomery, who met at the Carlton Hotel in early 1944 after watching amphibious landing rehearsals in Poole Bay.

At Bovington Camp in 1937, the RTC Central Schools had been replaced by the Army Armoured Fighting Vehicles School, and many new buildings were erected. On the formation of the Royal Armoured Corps in 1939, the RTC Depot became the RAC Depot, which was later replaced by 52nd (Heavy) Training Regiment RAC.

Infantry and Bren gun carriers of the 5th Battalion Northamptonsire Regiment pass through a village near Christchurch in March 1941 (IWM 7971).

Gunners of 20th Anti-Tank Regiment, 3rd Infantry Division haul a anti-tank gun up a slope during training at Verwood in March 1941 (IWM 8379).

Top Before going out on the open ranges, students at the Gunnery School were taught on Classroom Instuctional Mountings (skeletons of tank turrets containing all the necessary controls etc, linked to .22 calibre rifles, so that they could practise giving fire orders and other such drills, using small calibre ammunition.

Above Members of the ATS and local girls worked at the Command Workshops, Bovington, throughout the war.

A Light Tank on exercise near Bovington.

Training in tank crew trades was taught there and during the first year of the war it was joined by the 58th Training Regiment, specialising in tank commanders and officers training. Bovington also trained Canadians, Czechs and Poles. Lulworth Gunnery School grew likewise and as the war progressed, more and more land had to be taken over to cope with the ever changing needs of larger calibre tank guns. The Sea Danger area was expanded and first Heath Range, then Tyneham Valley in Worbarrow Bay, were acquired in 1943. By the end of the war a total of 35 different types of tank and armoured car had been taught at the AFV Schools.

Dorchester First Aid Post Centre was manned every day once the German bombing offensive started.

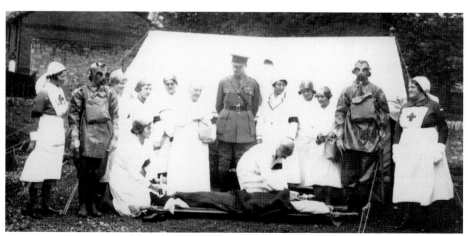

Commandos training at Osmington for the successful raid on a German radar post at Bruneval in 1942.

HERE COME THE YANKS!
THE FRIENDLY INVASION
1943 – 1944

Before the invasion of occupied Europe could begin, massive forces had to be assembled in the south of England. The planners split the south coast into two portions, roughly along the Dorset-Hampshire border. To the east would be mainly British and Canadians, to the west Americans, starting some nine months before D-Day. They came in waves – first those who would build the camps, hospitals and bases.

Then came the hospital staffs (at least seven hospitals were established, one of the main ones being the US Army 22nd General Hospital comprising five units, three at Blandford Camp and one each at Guy's Marsh and Kingston Lacy House. Each had 1,284 beds (raised to 1,400 in an emergency by the staff giving up their own beds). It 'opened for business' in April 1944. Casualties from Normandy were flown to Tarrant Rushton airfield and a special road was built to connect it to the hospital.

The first US Army unit to arrive at Blandford Camp (8 Dec 43) was 184 AA Gun Battalion, with the task of protecting the Studland Bay beach exercise area used to hone assault landing techniques, complete with naval gunfire, tanks and aircraft. The US Rangers (the American equivalent of our Commandos) did much of their specialist training on the loose limestone cliffs at Burton Bradstock and Swanage.

GIs relaxing with locals in a country pub. The photo was actually taken in the Dove Inn, Burton Bradstock, and the prominent poster for H & G Simmonds, brewers of Reading, was part of a deliberate plot to make the Germans believe that the troops who would invade France were based in the Home Counties and thus would strike at the Pas de Calais area and not Normandy.

A Booklet on Dorset

Every US Serviceman or woman coming to Dorset was issued with a small booklet about the county in which the Lord Lieutenant had written the following introduction:

A warm welcome awaits any members of the fighting services of the United States of America who may find themselves here in our midst in the County of Dorset. We would rejoice to think that they felt at home in our County and we would have them know that the hand of comradeship is at all times held out to our gallant allies and kinsmen. Anything that we in Dorset can do to strengthen the bonds of fellowship and the ties that bind us, will always be our first aim and endeavour.

Next to arrive were the troops destined to carry out the actual assault on the Normandy coast. Langton House, near Blandford, was occupied by HQ 1st US Infantry Division – known as 'The Big Red One' after their shoulder patch that had been adopted in the last days of the First World War. They were one of the finest divisions in the US Army (hence the saying that the US Army consisted of the Big Red One and ten million replacements!) and had already gained battle experience during the 'Operation Torch' landings in North Africa. They arrived in England from Sicily in November 1943 and stayed until D-Day in June 1944 . They comprised 34,142 men and 3,306 vehicles and together with the 29th (US) Infantry Division,

The Americans in Burton Bradstock. It was on the cliffs at Burton Bradstock that the American Rangers rehearsed their D-Day attack on the German guns controlling Utah and Omaha beaches.

would form the infantry element of US V Corps chosen as the D-Day assault force on Omaha Beach. The GIs quickly settled down to rural life, being widely spread throughout the county, mainly in 12 hutted and tented camps, but not all – for example, a plaque on the wall of Woodville House, Silver Street, Lyme Regis reads 'At this site Nov 1943 to June 1944 was located the headquarters of 'C' Co, 16th

The Americans brought out an illustrated guide to Bournemouth for GIs stationed there. The caption to this photograph read 'And you still want to go home?'.

Inf Reg, 1st US Inf Div who led the assault landing at Omaha Beach on D Day (June 6 1944) in Normandy France. Capt Victor H Briggs CO.'

The camps housed both British and American troops at some stage or another. Some were sealed prior to D-Day and the troops in them not allowed out whilst they were being briefed and making their final preparations, before moving down to the embarkation ports.

American troops making their way along Weymouth Esplanade before embarking for D-Day.

An American Army DUKW boards a LST (Landing Ship, Tank) prior to D-Day.

Other US divisions would spend shorter periods of time in Dorset, for example, US 4th Armored Division who had completed their pre-invasion training in Wiltshire, moved to the Dorchester area prior to loading in Southampton, Weymouth and Portland in early July 1944, whilst 99th US Infantry Division was stationed around Blandford during Oct-Nov 1944 and loaded at Weymouth, as did US 11th Armored Division, one of whose GIs in the column had a sobering experience:

'At one cottage I noticed a young woman with several small children huddled around her. Suddenly one small boy ran from her screaming at the top of his voice: "Mummy, Mummy, Daddy's come home!" He rushed into the street, crying for joy and threw his arms around one of my legs. His mother, tears in her eyes, came to retrieve him. "No love, not yet but some day he will", she almost pleaded as she comforted her small son. The incident made us all realise how much the British had already paid in the fight against common enemies.'

American troops of the 1st Division being packed into landing craft in Weymouth Harbour before D-Day. The two day crossing to Normandy in small boats was a nightmare . The flat-bottomed craft rolled badly, and for most the voyage was a mixture of seasickness, hunger, cramp, tiredness and nerves. The men in this photograph landed at dawn on Omaha beach, suffering the highest casualties of the invasion.

A farewell message chalked on a tent. The photograph was taken in one of the sealed camps left deserted when the GIs moved down to their embarkation ports. One wonders if Johnny ever returned to Jean.

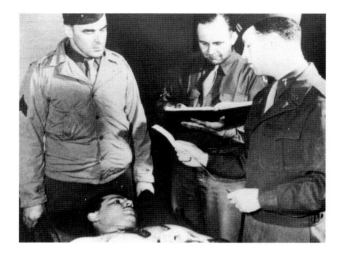

A wounded American soldier has his records checked on his arrival at the 22nd General Hospital, Blandford Camp, before being assigned to a ward.

The Casualties Arrive

It was not long before the American military hospitals in Dorset began to receive a steady stream of wounded from the beaches. The casualties who had already passed through the regimental aid posts and casualty clearing stations in France, were now transported quickly and efficiently to the general hospitals around Blandford. At times they were working to full capacity, with as many as 500 arriving in one evening. Five hospital trains operated in the southern counties, two being based at Bournemouth. Between D Day and 15 September 1944, the USNAAB Portland –Weymouth evacuated 26,390 dead and wounded US Army and Navy, British Army and Navy, prisoners of war and other personnel (including refugees) through the two ports of Portland and Weymouth.

1ST (US) INFANTRY DIVISION IN DORSET

DIVISIONAL STRENGTH as at 5 June 1944 – 34,142 men and 3,306 vehicles.

Division HQ
(Commander: Maj. Gen. Clarence R. Huebner)
Divisional Command Post – Langton House, near BLANDFORD FORUM. They arrived on 9 November 1943 and left on 2 June 1944, when the Command Post (Advanced) went on board *USS Ancon* and CP (Alternative) on board *USS Chase*.

16 Infantry Regiment
(Commander: Col. George A. Taylor)
Regimental Command Post – Parnham House, near BEAMINSTER.
The three infantry battalions, HQ Company, Service Company, Cannon Company and Anti-tank Company were all located in BRIDPORT, LYME REGIS, ABBOTSBURY, LITTON CHENEY and BEAMINSTER. Marshalling area before embarking: LONG BREDY.

18 Infantry Regiment
(Commander: Col. George A. Smith Jr)
Regimental Command Post – Ilsington House, near PUDDLETOWN.
1st Battalion – PIDDLEHINTON CAMP, then on 12 January 1944 to CHICKERELL CAMP.
2nd Battalion & Cannon Company – BROADMAYNE & WEST KNIGHTON.
3rd Battalion & Service Company – DORCHESTER.
Anti-tank Company – WINTERBORNE ST MARTIN.
HQ Company – PUDDLETOWN.

26 Infantry Regiment
(Commander: Col. John F. R. Seitz)
Regimental Command Post – Binnegar Hall, near WAREHAM.
1st & 2nd Battalions, Cannon Company & Anti-tank Company – SWANAGE.
3rd Battalion – BLANDFORD.
Service Company & HQ Company – WAREHAM.

1st Division Artillery
(Commander: Brig. Gen. Clift Andrus)
HQ & HQ Battery – SPETTISBURY.
Division Artillery (5th, 7th, 32nd & 33rd Field Artillery Battalions) – PIDDLEHINTON.

On 17 May 44, the HQ & HQ Battery left Spettisbury and was divided into four main groups:
Command Group No 1 with Force O under CG Div Arty,
Command Group No 2 with Force O under Div Arty S-3,
D-Day transportation with Force O under Arty Survey,
Remainder of battery with Force B under Bty Exec.

1st Engineer Combat Battalion
(Commander: Lt. Col. William B. Gara).
HQ & Svc Company – with Division HQ
Company A – CHARMOUTH
Company B – CORFE CASTLE
Company C – STUDLAND

1st Division Signal Company
(Commander: Maj. Leonard T. Peters)
Bryanston Camp, BLANDFORD.

1st Reconnaissance Troop
(Commander: Capt. William L. Blake)
Initially at Norden Hill Camp, MAIDEN NEWTON, then in PIDDLEHINTON CAMP.

1st Division MP Platoon
(Commander: Maj. Thomas F. Lancer)
Initially all in Camp D6 at PIDDLEHINTON, then dispersed to:
D6 – Piddlehinton (2 officers & 52 men)

D9 – WEYMOUTH (2 officers & 28 men)
Div HQ – BLANDFORD (l officer & 10 men)
rear echelon & in hospital – BOURNEMOUTH (4 men)

701st (Ordnance Light Maintenance Company
(Commander: Capt. Raymond C. Huntoon)
DORCHESTER. HQ in Wadham House, with 1st Platoon; 2nd Platoon in the Sunday school buildings of the Episcopal church; 3rd Platoon in the Barracks

1st Quartermaster Company
(Commander: Capt. John J. King)
DORCHESTER.

1st Medical Battalion
(Commander: Lt. Col. Samuel Bleichfield)
PIDDLEHINTON then to CATTISTOCK on 12 January 1944

VICTORY
1944 – 1945

Goodbye to Dad's Army

After D-Day it became clear that the enemy was never likely to invade the UK, so the Home Guard ceased to be needed. On 16 September 1944, it was announced that no more men would be directed into Home Guard service and that parades in future would be voluntary. 'Stand Down' came shortly afterwards on 1 November, but was not completed until 31 December 1944.

General Henry Jackson, who was then commanding the Dorset Home Guard, closed his farewell message with the words: 'The spirit of comradeship and service which was brought to life by service in the Dorset Home Guard must never be allowed to die.' Every man had, as the presentation certificate highlighted, given generously of his time and powers to make himself ready to defend his country by force of arms and with his life if necessary. This had been done, as one member succinctly put it with: 'No bands, no pay, no medals, no glory.'

At the time of the Stand Down, the Home Guard had a strength of 1,793,000 (of which 1,206 had died on duty). The cost to the country was just £9.25 per year per member, roughly equal to a single day's expenditure on the war effort. It was undoubtedly the cheapest army of its size and firepower that any nation ever possessed.

The Stand Down Parade of the 2nd (Dorset) Battalion of the Home Guard on a wintry December day in 1944. It took place in Dorchester, on the football field behind the Marabout Barracks. At its height, the Battalion strength rose to 1,900 men.

The Blackout Ends

Although the war would last for another complete year, the summer of 1944 brought a gradual relaxing of some of the myriad wartime restrictions and regulations. One of the most noticeable was the replacement on 17 September of the blackout with what was euphemistically called 'the dim-out', timed to coincide with the end of Double British Summertime. Not that it affected all of Dorset, as coastal areas to a depth of five miles inland were still restricted. Limited street lighting was switched on but with a much reduced lamp wattage. Windows needed only to be curtained, provided no direct light was visible from outside and in the event of an air raid street lights were switched off. It wasn't much, but at least it was a step towards normality.

There were still plenty of servicemen, both American and British in the county, so the clubs and voluntary organisations provided a 'home from home' for them. One of the highspots of the New Year festivities 1944/45 was a dance held at the American Red Cross Club in Weymouth attended by 500 GIs and their partners (ATS, Wrens, WAFs, nurses and local civilians) All had been issued with whistles to blow at midnight. However, it was reported that the assembled throng was making so much noise they could not be heard.

Recently arrived German prisoners of war are thoroughly searched at Portland POW cage.

Prisoners of War

Along with the casualties came captured enemy soldiers as one watcher recalled: 'In about September 1944, when the first batch of German POWs came into Castletown by LCT and were marched to the temporary POW camp on the rugby field just above Victoria Square. They were led by a senior officer, whom I was shocked to see was a woman abut the same age as my mother. They all smelt of earth and de-lousing powder. Any jingoistic urge to jeer was dispelled by their harmless and dejected appearance. I followed them to camp and offered one a cigarette, but a GI stopped me, saying that they got plenty from the guards.'

It should be noted that POW were still incarcerated until 1947, with Italians at Piddlehinton Camp and Germans at Park Camp, Lulworth. A pathetic reminder that these POWs were still in captivity two years after the war ended is supposed to have been painted on the road near the married quarters in large yellow letters: SEND US HOME!

Victory!

On VE Day (7 May 1945) in pubs and homes all over the county celebrations were in full swing, one commentator recalling: 'I can see the bar through the thick haze of smoke. The landlord and his wife are serving pints of beer as fast as they can draw them . . . there was Charles Battrick the thatcher, Trooper Clark on sick leave from Germany, Tom Woodsford a roadman, Charles Biggs a tractor driver, Jack Groves a shepherd, and old Herbie Chalk, a professional rabbit catcher, who may have done a bit of poaching! . . . you get the impression of things going on for ever the same . . . It is the England for which we have worked . . . Now we know we can pass on this blessed plot of earth to those who come after.'

ELEVEN

THE DORSETSHIRE REGIMENT
1939 – 1945

The 2nd Dorsets, then part of the 2nd Infantry Division, sailed over to France on 23 September 1939. As Hugh Popham comments: 'all that stood between them and the German Army, when they took up their position on the Franco-Belgian frontier a week or so later was a ditch with two feet of water in it and some concrete pill-boxes . . . the battalion spent a cold winter improving the defences on their section of the Maginot Line, with the minimum interference from the enemy. It was like being involved in a dream from which, one knew, one must eventually be woken.' The 'awakening' came on 9 April when Norway was invaded, then, just a month later, the 'Blitzkrieg' (Lightning War) was launched on the Western Front. By the end of June the BEF had been booted out of France and France had surrendered.

The 2nd Battalion had fought its first action near Ghoy, but just two days later they were out of Belgium and struggling to reach the one remaining open port of Dunkirk. They fought a stubborn and effective three day defensive battle on the La Bassee Canal, encircled by the Germans – whose divisional commander, General

Officers of the 1st Battalion, Dorsetshire Regiment, outside the Depot Barracks in 1939. The Battalion landed in France on D-Day and much later formed part of the first infantry patrol to cross into Germany.

Rifle inspection for men of the 2nd Battalion, Dorsetshire Regiment at Rumegies, France, 14 February 1940 (IWM F 2572).

Erwin Rommel (later nicknamed the 'Desert Fox') reported the situation as being 'extremely critical'. The 2nd Dorsets were ordered to hold Festubert, then carry out a fighting withdrawal which they did, repulsing every attack and then 'slipping away' across country. After a hair-raising night, the remaining 250 men reached Doulieu where they learned that the BEF was to be evacuated. For two more days they helped to hold the Furnes Canal on the Dunkirk perimeter, then, on the night of 30 May, they marched, under fire but still with their personal weapons, onto the mole and aboard a dredger, safely reaching Margate Pier the next morning.

Having survived with honour, they spent the next eighteen months manning coastal defences in Yorkshire, then in the autumn of 1941 received sailing orders which were immediately cancelled – fortunately as it turned out, because the replacement battalion was taken prisoner in Singapore. The 2nd did not leave the UK (bound for India) until the spring of 1942.

The 1st Battalion was on Malta when war started – part of the Malta Brigade, living in almost peacetime conditions, until Italy entered the war when the island came under siege. The enemy tried to neutralise the island with heavy bombing, whilst the garrison was fully engaged manning the defences, building aircraft pens, repairing runways, manning light Ack Ack guns, not to mention unloading, vital supplies from any ships that still got through. The siege effectively ended after the Battle of Alamein in October 1942, and in March 1943, 231, the Malta Brigade, (2nd Devons, 1st Hants and 1st Dorsets) sailed to Alexandria to begin three months of strenuous rehearsal prior to the invasion of Sicily.

When the 2nd Battalion sailed from UK in April 1942 they hoped they were heading for North Africa, but instead ended up in India, where it would be almost two years before they would see action. However, they were kept extremely busy carrying out exacting training, so they were well prepared for the action that would follow. It began in April 1944, as the Japanese completed their three-week, 100 mile, advance up the Manipur Road to invest Imphal and Kohima, with the aim of sweeping on to take Dimapur and cut the Bengal Assam railway. Almost immediately, the battalion was on its way to recover Kohima. The battle that followed over the next three weeks was hard fought, despite the fact that the objectives were tiny – the District Commissioner's bungalow and tennis court, whilst the opposing sides were less than 50 yards apart most of the time. The enemy were well dug-in with carefully positioned field guns that were able to sweep every approach line.

Sniped at and mortared from every angle, on a battlefield constantly pervaded by the overpowering stench of rotting flesh, flies, monsoon rains and incessant heat, the Dorsets and all the rest grimly fought a hand to hand battle, the first attack being made on 26/27 April by A Company of the Dorsets. They managed to slip past the Jap positions and dug in close to the DCs bungalow. The cliff, now being held by A Coy, commanded the junction of three vital roads, thus enabling future attacks to be developed. They managed to hold on there for a week before being relieved, only 28 of the original 100 returning unscathed. It was eventually decided that the only answer would be to get a tank up there and, despite the difficulty, this was achieved on 12 May and the position finally taken. 74 men of the battalion had died during the previous 19 days. Nevertheless it would be a further three weeks before the enemy were finally driven off Kohima Ridge and the pursuit could begin. To quote Hugh Popham again: 'on June 18 the battalion, having advanced 16 miles in the day, crossed the frontier into Burma and thus added 'Primus ex Indis' unofficially to the Regiment's honours.' In playing its part at Kohima, a battle now regarded as one of the most decisive in the war in the Far East, the battalion had lost 473 all ranks killed, wounded, died or sick.

Meanwhile, the 1st Battalion was on its way to Sicily for its first assault landing just north of Cape Passaro on 10 July 1943. They met little opposition and soon had achieved all their immediate objectives. 'During the ensuing three weeks they marched and fought their ways to the very foothills of Mount Etna. "These Tommies fight well", a German officer confided to his diary.'

From Sicily the brigade went on to land in Italy that September, first setting foot on mainland Europe on the 8th. A few days later the brigade was taken out of the line and then heard that they were going back to UK – over six years after they had originally left home. They were now part of 50th (Northumbrian) Division involved in combined operations exercises, firstly on the East Coast, then at Inverary, Studland Bay ('home' ground' in Dorset) and Hayling Island. Then,

The grainy photograph and strain on the faces says it all.
The 1st Dorsets heading for Utah Beach early on D-Day.

on 31 May the battalion began to embark on the *Empire Spearhead* and *Empire Crossbow*, bound for the Normandy beaches and on through the rest of German-held Europe, through which the three Dorset battalions (1st, 4th and 5th) would fight their way to eventual victory with considerable distinction.

Early on the morning of 6 June 1944, the 1st Dorsets and 1st Hants shared the honour of being the first two battalions to land in France, making their way ashore at Le Hamel on Utah Beach. Despite a strong German defence inflicting reasonably heavy casualties, they rapidly fought their way inland, captured Point 54 and by last light had taken all their initial objectives. These included Arromanches which had been selected for the construction of the first Mulberry Harbour. The total 1st Battalion casualties on D-Day were 128 all ranks.

For the next few days, the Dorsets were part of the van and together with 8th Armoured Brigade, they took and held 'Tiger Hill', fighting against the crack 12th Panzer Division. The 'bocage' countryside with its sunken roads and high hedgerows favoured the enemy, the Dorsets suffering over 100 casualties including

Universal carriers of 50th Division, carrying the 1st Dorsets, go ashore on D-Day from landing craft on Utah Beach.

their CO killed. This was also a time when great storms did their best to wreck the Mulberry Harbour. The troops who had landed on D-Day had now been fighting without respite ever since and were fast becoming exhausted. Nevertheless, there would be a month of almost 'Static Slogging' before the virtual destruction of the German 7th and 15th Armies in the Falaise Pocket. This was a period of hard patrolling and some savage fighting, which began when they took Villers Bocage and ended a week later at Pierre-La-Vieille. The battle for Normandy was now won and the second phase of the invasion completed.

The 4th and 5th Battalions had landed at Arromanches in the last week of June and were soon in action. After three weeks in the line the 4th were withdrawn for a rest, but were soon back in the thick of it. When the break-out came in August, the 43rd Division headed due east to the Seine, crossing the river at Vernon and Vernonne on the 27th. They continued through Belgium in what is best described as a 'triumphal procession', with liberated villagers and townsfolk everywhere, rushing out to cover them with flowers, fruit, kisses and wine.

With the Seine crossing now secure, the Guards Armoured Division passed through to make a dash from Picardy and on into Belgium – leaving the Wessex Division without transport for two weeks. Nevertheless, by 12 September, the Dorsets had reached the outskirts of Brussels, where the 4th Battalion discovered a German wine store that kept them supplied with champagne for many days to come! The

Men of the 5th Battalion, Dorsetshire Regiment, crossing the Rhine into Germany in a Buffalo, 28 March 1945 (IWM BU 2449).

1st Battalion then veered off northwards towards Antwerp, Merxem and the Albert and Escaut canals. Here, the 4th would achieve fame in Operation Market Garden – a complex and daring attempt to capture the river crossings at Arnhem, Nijmegen, Eindhoven and Grave, so as to turn the enemy defence line along the Rhine and thus cut off over 100,000 German troops in Holland. The story is almost a legend now, the epic work of the 4th Dorsets on the night of 24 September being an important part. They were ordered to cross the Neder Rijn to the south-west of Arnhem to cover the evacuation of 1st Airborne survivors. They made their way under heavy enemy fire against a strong current and in leaky boats. Some 300 of the battalion made it across, then held out for 36 hours, while 2,400 paratroopers were ferried back. Few of the 4th made the nightmare return journey, their bravery being acknowledged specifically by Montgomery, when he wrote in *Normandy to the Baltic*: 'Other detachments of the Dorsets were left on the north bank of the river still fighting in a most gallant manner to cover the operation.' Post-war the 4th Battalion would be presented with a 1st Airborne flag in remembrance of their bravery.

Other actions included those by the 5th Battalion actions at Bauchem and Dorset Wood in the Sittard triangle – later taken over by the 4th who held the wet miserable shell-blasted trenches for eight terrible days. About this time the 1st Battalion claimed another 'first', when one of their foot patrols crossed the German border near Beek at 1635 hours on 29 September – the first British infantry to set foot in Germany!

Men of the 2nd Battalion, Dorsetshire Regiment, pass a knocked out Lee tank as they make their way to their way to the foot of Mount Popa, Burma, 20 April 1945 (IWM SE 3859).

Mid-December would see the Germans launching their Ardennes offensive, both the 4th and 5th Battalions being alerted but not involved, whilst the 1st had already been sent back to UK to join 50th Division, there to utilise their years of battle experience in training others.

The 'Battle of the Bulge' in the Ardennes was over by early February 1945 and the Allies had resumed their assault into Germany across the Rhine, culminating in the elimination of all enemy forces west of the Rhine and the breaching of the Siegfried Line's outer defences. Both battalions were following up the initial assault and quickly took their immediate objectives. By the beginning of May they had passed Bremen and were soon advancing towards Cuxhaven. The 4th fought their last engagement at Glinstedt and two days later it was all over, as their history puts it: 'The Higher Commanders had their impressive ceremonies of surrender but for the private soldier the war had just fizzled out.'

The war in Europe was over, but the fighting against the Japanese was still going on, the next major obstacle being the mighty 1,500 yards-wide, fast flowing Irrawaddy, with the Japanese dug in on the far bank and few serviceable boats. However, having crossed the river with some difficulty, they were soon on their way again in a final, concerted 40 mile drive, cross-country to Mandalay which was reached on 20 March. Their final task was to assault the strongly-held plateau below Mount Popa. They had covered, mostly on foot, some 700 miles of jungle, leaving behind just a multitude of white crosses and the now famous memorial at Kohima: 'When you go home, tell them of us and say: For your tomorrow, we gave our today.'

TWELVE

THE RIFLES

The process of amalgamation that led to the creation of the Devonshire and Dorset Regiment in 1958 did not mark an end to the changes. Indeed, one of the most significant of all happened only recently. In 2007, after completing their last operational tour in Iraq, the Regiment joined with three others to form 'The Rifles'. This youngest of all Army regiments celebrated its official first birthday on 1st February 2008 and has already begun to forge an excellent reputation, both in the Army and in the wider civilian community.

As Lt Col Geoff Nicholls has written in a series of excellent articles in recent issues of the annual *Dorset Year Book*, 'We are trying hard to be regarded as the county regiment of Dorset . . . The first thing which most people will notice is that the Regiment wears green, rather than khaki uniforms. This came about, perhaps surprisingly, because of a Dorset connection through Colonel Coote Manningham who joined the 39th (later the Dorset Regiment) as a junior officer in 1782. In 1800 he became the first commanding officer of the Corps of Experimental Riflemen, known as Manningham's Sharpshooters, who, to aid camouflage, dressed in green uniforms. What might seem like commonsense today was a controversial move away from the century-long tradition of red jackets. He was known as 'the father of thinking Riflemen' and a popular song of the day went thus:

Oh! Colonel Coote Manningham, he was the man,
For he invented a capital plan,
He raised a Corps of Riflemen
To fight for England's glory!

He dressed them all in jackets of green
And placed them where they couldn't be seen
And sent in front, an invisible screen
To fight for England's glory!

The Rifles uniform recognizes the Light Infantry heritage that required them to move speedily around the battlefield. Speed of movement also meant that they dispensed with items that would encumber them – so drums, the traditional method of communication in the infantry, were replaced by bugles. Colours

The Rifles being applauded as they march through Dorchester in September 2007 during their first Freedom Parade (Crown copyright).

would certainly be out of place in this environment, so it was decided that they would be carried by all ranks – in the form of a belt badge displaying former battle honours. These traditions live on in the uniform of the new regiment – the bugle being the new cap-badge and the belt badge being worn by senior NCOs, warrant officers and officers.'

The Rifles now (in 2011) comprises seven battalions in all, five regular (1-5) and two territorial (6 and 7), based as follows: 1st – Chepstow; 2nd – Ballykinler (N. Ireland); 3rd – Edinburgh; 4th – Bulford; 5th – Paderborn; 6th – HQ in Exeter with companies in Gloucester, Taunton, Truro and Dorchester; 7th – HQ in Reading with companies in Milton Keynes, Oxford and London. They have three bands, one with each TA battalion and one regular, based in Winchester. The Salamanca Band of 6th Rifles has already performed quite frequently in Dorset. The Regiment is fully manned, one of few in this enviable state of affairs. In addition to adult soldiers almost all members of the Army Cadet Force in Dorset wear the Rifles' cap badge.

The 6th Battalion is the battalion most relevant to Dorset, for it includes elements of the 4th Battalion Devonshire and Dorsets originally part of the Rifle Volunteers. HRH The Duke of Edinburgh is Colonel in Chief of the Rifles, whilst each battalion has a Royal Colonel – the 6th's being HRH The Duke of Gloucester.

Regimental activities in Dorset are looked after by two designated Rifles senior officers (a brigadier who looks after all the south-west counties and a Lieutenant Colonel exclusively for Dorset). Recent activities have included 'freedom' or 'homecoming' parades through Blandford, Bournemouth, Dorchester, Poole, Shaftesbury, Weymouth and Wimborne Minster. All the ceremonies have included the exchange of a Freedom Scroll and Silver Bugle, and have helped to bind the Regiment to their places of origin – their counties, cities and towns.

A soldier from the 2nd Rifles Battlegroup on foot patrol in Kosovo in 2008 (Crown copyright).

Recent Operations

All seven battalions have been involved in operations in either Iraq or Afghanistan, indeed some have taken part in their second operational tour – 'such is the pace of life in the battalions whether they are regular or territorial' comments Col Geoff Nicholls in the latest *Dorset Year Book* for 2010. He goes on to explain what each battalion has been doing and closes with the words 'There is no doubt this has been just about as demanding a year as could be imagined for the Regiment, but Riflemen in all battalions have risen to the challenges admirably.'

His article thus gives a perfect snapshot of operations in 2009, from which he has kindly allowed me to quote. The 1st Battalion began 2009 training in Belize, later going to Afghanistan to provide Operational Mentoring and Liaison Teams (OMLTS, otherwise known as omlettes!) for the Afghan National Army (ANA). 'Life was tough, with facilities in patrol bases being extremely basic, while patrolling was inherently dangerous. Much of the 'green zone' of thick vegetation along the Helmand River provided havens of close cover for the enemy who took every opportunity to attack; often with rifles, machine guns and rocket propelled grenades, but increasingly with improvised explosive devices (IEDs). Despite the dangers and frustrations, most members of the battalion felt that they had achieved a great deal during their six month tour. Certainly it was not without cost, with the loss of seven members of the battalion killed in action.

'The 2nd Battalion had expected to deploy on exercise to Kenya in early 2008,

Much of the recent service of the Rifles has been in Iraq and Afghanistan. The photograph above shows them on patrol with the 1st Mechanised Brigade near Basra in Iraq, the one below in Sangin Province, Afghanistan, in 2009 (Crown copyright).

'but events conspired to send them to a cold Salisbury Plain followed by a rather warmer Kosovo for two months during the potentially difficult period of the country's move to independence. This proved to be reasonable preparation for the forthcoming operational tour in Afghanistan and was followed by' further training, some of it at a 'rather rundown camp on the edge of Salisbury Plain, meant to replicate Sangin. Their deployment in April 2009 coincided with the return of the 1st Battalion, although their respective roles and areas of responsibility were mostly quite different. 2nd Battalion became Battle Group North, further up the Helmand River than 1st Battalion and working from company camps known as Forward Operating Bases (FOBs), including one much further north at Kajaki where the river is dammed.'

The 3rd Battalion had a varied year, with a company deploying to Kosovo throughout the latter half of 2008 and another to the Falklands. 2009 has seen the whole battalion on training exercises in Kenya, the first stage of preparation for their move to Afghanistan in the autumn, as the 2nd Battalion returns.

'The 4th Battalion returned from Iraq at the end of 2007, where they were the last soldiers in central Basra, and spent much of 2008 conducting conventional training, particularly re-training on their Bulldog armoured vehicles, culminating in a large exercise on Salisbury Plain, after which the Battalion reverted to operating on foot as part of the Small Scale Focused Intervention (SSFI) Battlegroup ready to deploy anywhere at a drop of the hat. Their first role was to cover the 2009 summer elections in Afghanistan, a task involving two companies – effectively half the battalion. Tragically they lost two soldiers early in their tour.'

The 5th Battalion are equipped with Warrior armoured fighting vehicles and as such are known as an Armoured Infantry Battalion. Although they are able to train in Europe, by far the largest and best training area for armoured vehicles is in Alberta, Western Canada. Just days after arriving there in 2008, they were hit by a snowstorm – the worst for almost a century. Hardly ideal preparation for the next challenge, preparing for and deploying to Iraq! By a twist of fate they were one of the last battalions to pull out of that troubled country, having been one of the first to deploy there in 2003 and having conducted two tours there in between. There is no doubt at all that the city of Basra is a better place now than it was six years ago and all the soldiers who have been on operations there can be proud of what has been achieved.'

'It might be considered that a Territorial battalion would have a less demanding time than its regular counterparts. Not so, as far as the 6th Battalion were concerned. The battalion deployed a company of 100 men to Afghanistan for six months from autumn 2008 to the following spring. As well as carrying out base security around Camp Bastion, they were able to carry out a number of tasks in the Helmand River valley. Meanwhile the beginning of the period saw the 7th Battalion welcoming home yet more Afghan veterans: 'this time in the shape of Salonika Company, who, like their 6th Battalion counterparts, had spent six months in Helmand Province.'

2010 has been the toughest to date in the Rifles short history, 34 officers and soldiers being killed in action in Afghanistan and many more seriously wounded. However, to quote Colonel Nicholls again: 'Strange as it may seem to those not intimately involved, this sacrifice has helped to forge the Rifles into a much more

The Rifles training for a beach landing in 2008 (Crown copyright).

closely-knit unit than might have been possible if the circumstances had been different.'

At the time of writing (mid 2011) the 1st Battalion are back in Afghanistan as part of 3 Commando Brigade. They have found Helmand Province a very different place to the one they left two years ago, with much progress having been made towards relative normality. There are still inherent dangers from enemy activity, but the area's infrastructure is on a much more solid foundation and most members of the population are becoming openly more supportive of the British troop. But there is still much to be done and in the autumn the 2nd and 5th Battalions take over responsibility for security in the area. It is not long before the 2014 deadline when British forces are to withdraw and the pressure is on to ensure that the Afghan Army and Police Force are ready to take over. Consequently, more and more effort is being put into training the Afghans – indeed, that is to be the 2nd Battalion's main effort.

In the meantime the 3rd and 4th Battalions, although not officially warned for further operational tours, are fairly certain that they will be required and have recently conducted tough, and entirely appropriate, training in the heat and dust of Kenya in between periods of high readiness for any worldwide crisis which would require their presence – a role called Spearhead Lead Element. The Territorials of the 6th and 7th Battalions continue to prove their worth by providing scores of soldiers to boost the numbers of the regular battalions on operations. The Regiment as a whole is fully recruited and has forged a fine reputation over the past 5 years. Whatever changes happen to the Army under the various reviews being undertaken, The Rifles are in the strongest possible position not just to survive, but to thrive.

THIRTEEN
POST-WAR: BARRACKS AND MEMORIALS

Considering the impact that the Second World War had on Dorset, there is fortunately not much tangible evidence of it left. The bomb damage has long been repaired, fortifications and beach defences have been removed or softened by nature. Here and there you may find a dilapidated pillbox, the remains of a 'dragons teeth' anti-tank obstacle, or even some rusting barbed wire. It is in the military museums, on the town and village war memorials and in the places of worship with the laid up regimental colours that its legacy can best be found.

The large and important military camps remain – such as Bovington, Lulworth and Blandford – with a bewilderingly new range of occupants, whilst some smaller camps have gone over to civilian occupation. What rightly survive are the names of the fallen on war memorials the length of the county – one of the most striking being Eric Gill's dramatic cross at the end of Bladen Valley in Briantspuddle. There are also a few special larger items such as the pink granite obelisk in the Borough Gardens, Dorchester, dedicated to the NCOs and men who were killed or died of wounds during the Tirah campaign on the NW Frontier in 1897–98. The largest must be the Roosevelt Memorial Park, located inside Blandford Camp, dedicated to the American soldiers who gave their lives in the Second World War – to quote Colonel Fourrier's opening words at the dedication ceremony, which are now inscribed on a six foot tall obelisk: 'A plot of soil in England that is forever America.'

The dedication of the Roosevelt Memorial Park, Blandford Camp, in May 1945.

The end of the Depot Barracks, Dorchester. The Barracks closed in 1958 when the Regimental Headquarters moved to Exeter. Two years later the buildings were sold to Dorset County Council and the Royal Mail, whilst the Keep was retained as the Regimental Museum.

In cathedrals, abbeys and churches hang the fading Regimental Standards of the Regiments that have been laid up in the normal manner – so for example, the old colours of the wartime battalions of the Dorset Regiment now hang in Sherborne Abbey, together with those of past, disbanded Dorset battalions. The Regiment also has a memorial chapel there. Some locations are more unexpected – like the Union Flag and Regimental Standard of the 2nd Searchlight Regiment, RA, that were laid up in Cranborne Parish Church on 20 May 1990, whilst many items in use in the church today were presented by the Regiment's Reunion Association.

THE WESSEX DIVISION MEMORIAL

A replica of the divisional memorial which stands on Hill 112 near Caen, Normandy, is also to be found in Dorset – at Rough Tor, Winyard's Gap, on the A356 Dorchester to Crewkerne road. There is another such memorial in Wessex at Castle Hill, Mere, north of Shaftesbury. The divisional memorial roll is in the memorial chapel at Salisbury Cathedral.

BOVINGTON AND LULWORTH CAMPS

Before dealing with the current occupants of Bovington and Lulworth Camps, it is necessary to explain briefly what has happened there since the war ended. 'I changed the title of this place from Central Schools, Bovington Garrison, to HQ RAC Centre eighteen months ago', wrote General Nigel Duncan in his handover notes of August 1949, 'I did this quite deliberately to foster a sense of unity among the people who live here and I think it has had a certain effect. I have continual

89

Gun cleaning in progress on a Chieftain tank outside the tank hangars at Lulworth.

trouble with outsiders who do not understand that the RAC Centre comprises the Schools, the Depot, Workshop, Hospital etc and persist in using the title as if it applied only to the Schools.' As we shall see, those who took over changed its name yet again – now it is called simply 'The Armour Centre'.

Other major changes, such as major units arriving in the early post-war days were as follows: the RAC Depot returned to Bovington from County Durham in January 1947; the following year 3 RTR moved into Bovington Camp, to be followed by 7 RTR. Neither came to provide soldiers to help run the RAC Centre as would be the case some years later, but rather just to make use of the barracks, before moving on to the Far East. Two other important arrivals that stayed longer were the Boys Squadron, RAC that came into existence in January 1952 and would go on to become the highly successful RAC Junior Leaders Regiment, now sadly disbanded. Another new unit to arrive in the 1950s was the School of Tank Technology (STT) from Chobham in November 1951. Its main task was to give technical training to regimental officers in such matters as AFV design. They ran three main long courses: Mechanical, Gunnery and later, Guided Weapons. Their secondary task was to provide the Director, RAC, with technical advice. In 1966, it was redesignated as the Armour School, but has since been disbanded.

The 1960s were also the decade when more rebuilding was begun in Bovington and Lulworth than at any time since the beginning of the First World War. It covered new married quarters on the camp fringes, new batchelor quarters in or near the new messes and amenities for the soldiers and their families such as clubs and shops, whilst most of the instructional facilities were also renewed. The RAC Memorial Hall and a new Garrison church were also included, whilst in 1965, the Junior Leaders Regiment moved into the newly-built Stanley Barracks, Bovington, which had been tailor-made for them and taken five years to complete. During the 1970s and 1980s ten RAC Regiments carried out the duties of RAC Centre Regiment, each tour lasting about two years, their tasks being many and varied. Perhaps the most ambitious part of the rebuild of Bovington Camp – certainly the largest single building – was the opening of a new Workshop on the site of the existing 18 Command Workshop, REME on 3 June 1985. The 'star' of the proceedings was the new Challenger 1 main battle tank which went on to see action in the Gulf Wars. Lulworth too had its workshops rebuilt in the 1980s.

LULWORTH RANGE WALKS

One of the most emotive issues was settled in the early 1970s, namely public access to the tank gunnery ranges around Lulworth Camp. As we have seen, large areas of strikingly beautiful coastal land around the Gunnery Schools had been taken over and then purchased during and after the Second World War so that it could be used for military training, in particular live firing. Undoubtedly the area that epitomised the most energetic crusade over the years to 'Get the Army out!' has been the Tyneham Valley. But there was an equally vocal, locally-backed 'Keep the Army in Lulworth' crusade, that appreciated what damage would be done to the local economy and to the combat readiness and efficiency of the Army should they leave. Fortunately, a sensible compromise was reached, allowing public access during non-firing periods, along specially cleared paths (the Lulworth Range Walks). Those who cleared these paths were a charming group of displaced men from the Ukraine, who were specially trained members of the Royal Engineers Bomb Disposal Branch – thanks to them the paths were carefully cleared, 'finds' being defused and blown up nearby. Eventually the paths had all been cleared, marked and were ready for opening to the public. They have proved

The Purbeck village of Tyneham as it is today.

to be highly successful. They are now looked after, the public advised and the wildlife safeguarded, by a specially-trained team of Range Wardens. Interestingly, there is a greater concentration of wildlife inside the range area than in most of the official nature reserves in the county. There is also a significant 'Sea Danger Area' which is closed to shipping when firing is in progress and finally, an ever-watchful radar station on the top of Bindon Hill.

BLANDFORD CAMP

Following the vacation of the camp by the American hospital personnel during the latter part of 1945, Blandford Camp remained empty whilst the huts were reconverted from their use as specialised hospital premises. The first unit to re-enter the transformed camp was 1st Searchlight Regiment, RA, later to become a National Service training regiment for those called up to serve in the RA. They occupied Craddock Lines and were later joined in 1947 by a similar NS training unit of the RASC in Anson and Drake Lines. 1948 saw them depart and in their place No 1 Training Battalion REME arrived in 1948 and later, the ACC opened a Cookery Instruction Centre that would remain until 1962.

During 1948 and continuing until the early 1960s, the camp became well known as a site for motorcycle racing, a report in *Motor Cycle Racing* magazine commenting that races there drew large crowds that averaged 30,000 people at each meeting.

The Royal Corps of Signals Arrive

During April 1960, the first Royal Signals unit – 30th Signal Regiment – moved into Evans Lines and the following month, the Regiment marched through the town of Blandford Forum, the salute being taken by the Mayor. This would be the start of R Signals training at Blandford Camp, and their presence grew larger as National Service ended and the RASC, REME and ACC training units were gradually phased out. Later in the 1960s it was decided to move the School of Signals from Catterick Camp in Yorkshire to Blandford, but before this could happen much of the old wooden-hutted camp had to be demolished and be replaced by new, modern, permanent buildings. As at Bovington many new buildings were erected both for administrative and instructional purposes, including for example, no fewer than 70 plus married quarters.

In June 1970, on the fiftieth anniversary of the formation of the Royal Corps of Signals (formed from the Signals Service of the Royal Engineers in June 1920), the Signals began the move to Blandford. Two years later, in 1972, the centenary year of the arrival of their forebears in the area, the Royal Corps of Signals was granted the Freedom of Blandford Forum, and they have since became a familiar sight in Dorset, and are often seen training on verges and in lanes.

Top A signaller operating a TAC SAT terminal in Iraq.

Above Royal Signals soldiers setting up communications at a forward operating base in Afghanistan during Operation Herrick.

They Royal Corps of Signals are one of the British Army's vital combat support arms, supplying full telecommunications wherever it operates. It is thus responsible for the installing, operating and maintaining of all types of telecommunications equipment (including voice, data and satellite) and for providing support to commanders and their headquarters. They also conduct electronic warfare against enemy communications (including both electronic warfare and electronic counter measures). Since the end of the Second World they have played a full and active part in all campaigns, including Palestine, Aden, Cyprus, Indonesia and Malayasia, the Falklands, Sierra Leone, Bosnia and Kosovo, the 1st and 2nd Gulf Wars and are currently operational in Afghanistan.

FOURTEEN

MILITARY MUSEUMS

Undoubtedly the most important archives of military information in the county are housed in the four military museums, located in Dorchester, Blandford. Bovington and Weymouth.

The Keep Military Museum, Dorchester, covers all the county regiments past and present, both infantry and cavalry, from the 1700s onwards. The artefacts, weapons, uniforms, medals and of course the stories of the soldiers and their families, etc are on display on three floors of the Keep. To quote from their leaflet; 'Within these walls rests a history of the bravery and valour of men and women of Devon & Dorset.' Unique items on display include Adolf Hitler's desk, 'acquired' by the Dorsets from Hitler's Chancellery in Berlin.

The Royal Corps of Signals Museum, Blandford Camp, has displays dealing with the history of army communications dating from the Crimean War to present day. There are also various types of signals vehicles, motor cycles, and a selection of uniforms. Other exhibits show the development of military telegraph, telephone and radio, including a unique collection of WW2 spy radios. Also housed are the Corps medal collection and a small gallery showing the history of Blandford Camp. The museum now also highlights the heroic role of 'Women at War', with permanent displays featuring the ATS, SOE, FANY and the WRAC.

The Tank Museum (Royal Armoured Corps and Royal Tank Regiment Museums), Bovington, houses the largest collection of armoured fighting vehicles in the world, featuring tanks from all over the globe that fought in two World Wars and other major conflicts. Constantly expanding, this world-renowned museum puts on numerous action-packed live displays, whilst its static exhibits range from the first tank ever built to the modern-day Challenger main battle tank. Supplementary displays cover every aspect of armoured soldiering and explain every facet of the life of a tank crewman. Excellent customer facilities include a picnic area, licensed restaurant, shop, library and archive, etc.

The Museum of Coastal Defence is housed in the Nothe Fort, Weymouth. This fort was built by the Victorians to help protect Portland Harbour and is one of the best preserved forts of it type in the UK. There are some 30+ displays, many with sound and movement, exhibits and audio-visual facilities on the Ramparts, Gun Decks and in the maze of underground passageways. The views of Weymouth and Portland harbours from the battlements are spectacular. Lifts & ramps provide access to all the main areas of the Fort.

Above Every year the Tank Museum at Bovington holds a summer weekend 'Tank fest'.

Left A display in the Signals Museum, Blandford.

Below left In the entrance to the Keep Military Museum, Dorchester, is a display showing Lt Blaksley during the 1916 charge at Agagia. He had two horses killed under him and was awarded the Miltary Cross.

Below The Nothe Fort Volunteers at Weymouth fire the noonday gun during one of their regular displays.

FURTHER READING

Bishop, Terry, *The Dorsetshire Regiment*, 1999

Churchill, Colin, *Dorchester versus Hitler, A Country Town goes to War*, 2006

Forty, George & Anne, *Women War Heroines*, 1997
  Bovington Tanks, 1988

Forty, George, *Frontline Dorset: A County at War 1939-45*, 1994

Glyn, Maj. Richard H., *A short account of the Queen's Own Dorset Yeomanry 1794-1939*, QODY Old Comrades Association.

Harfield, Alan, *Blandford and the Military*, 1984

Heaning, Tony – (editor) *Dorchester Divided*

Legg, Rodney, *Dorset – America*, 2006
  Dorset at War – Diary of WW2, 1986

Lello, John, *Lyme Regis Past*, 1999

Morris, Stuart, *Portland, An Illustrated History*, 1998

Pearce, Robin, *Dorset Attacked – Dorset Defended*, 1999
  Seven Months to D-Day, 2000

Pomeroy, Colin, 'Discover Dorset', *Castles & Forts*, 1998
  Military Dorset Today, 1995

Popham, Hugh, *The Dorset Regiment*, 1970

Radnor, John, *It all happened before, the Home Guard through the Ages*, 1945

ACKNOWLEDGEMENTS

I am grateful to the following for their help, both with the text and the illustrations: Steven Booth, the Nothe Fort Museum of Coastal Defence; Valerie Dicker, Dorset County Museum; Adam Forty, The Royal Corps of Signal Museum; Rita O'Donoghue, The Imperial War Museum; Lt Col (Retd) Philip James, TD, Chairman QODY & DG Association; David Jenkins, Dorset County Council; Roger Lowless; Lt Col (Retd) Stephen May, MOD; Regt Col RTR; Lt Col (Retd) Geoff Nicholls, Rifles Secretary, Exeter; Capt Colin Parr, MBE, The Keep Military Museum; John Pidgeon; Peter Pitman, Editor *Dorset Year Book*; Poole Museums Service, Mrs Janice Tait, Librarian, The Tank Museum; Shane Wilkinson, Army Media & Communication.